혼공 기초 구문

혼공 기초 구문

허준석·신영환 지음

L3

혼공
혼공북스

혼공 기초 구문 Level 3

1판 1쇄 2022년 2월 7일
1판 2쇄 2024년 4월 1일

지은이 허준석 신영환
디자인 박새롬
표지그림 김효지
마케팅 두잉글 사업 본부
브랜드 혼공북스
펴낸곳 혼공북스
출판등록 제2021-000288호
주 소 04033 서울특별시 마포구 양화로 113 4층(서교동)
전자메일 team@hongong.co.kr

ISBN 979-11-976810-2-8 13740

머리말

혼공!

눈앞에 맛있는 소고기가 있어요. 너무 배고파서 바로 먹고 싶은데 고기가 너무 커서 한 입에 넣을 수가 없어요. 이럴 때 어떻게 해야 하죠?

맞아요. 작게 잘라서 한 입에 쏘옥 넣어서 먹으면 되지요.

영어 읽기도 마찬가지예요. 긴 영어 글을 한방에 읽고 핵심만 쏙쏙 이해하고 싶잖아요? 하지만 긴 글을 한 호흡에 읽어나가는 것은 쉽지가 않아요. 그렇기 때문에 쌤이 말한 소고기의 원리를 적용해 봅시다. 글을 한 입에 들어갈 수 있을 정도의 작은 단위로 잘라보는 거예요. 그 적당한 크기를 보통 문장이라고 하지요.

이렇게 영어 글을 문장 단위로 잘라서 공부하는 것을 구문공부 또는 구문독해라고 해요. 원서 읽기를 술술술 해내는 친구들에게는 필요가 없을 수도 있지만, 한국에서 자란 많은 친구들에게는 한 번쯤 꼬옥 해볼 것을 권한답니다.

특히 문장을 공부하면서 그 속에서 나오는 단어, 문법을 익히고, 우리말을 보면서 영작까지 해본다면 독해는 물론, 수행평가, 지필고사의 기본기까지 한 번에 쌓을 수 있어요.

우리 친구들! 영어는 절대 어렵지 않아요. 선생님과 함께 딱 20일 동안 교재, 강의를 충실히 보고 나면 자신감이 생길 거예요. 걱정말고 즐겁게, 효율적으로 혼공 해봅시다.
이제 준비되었나요? 그럼 다 같이 Let's get it!

대표저자 | 혼공 허준석

〈혼공기초구문 레벨 3〉 미리보기

총 ④단계의 완공, 혼공 시스템!

1 혼공기초

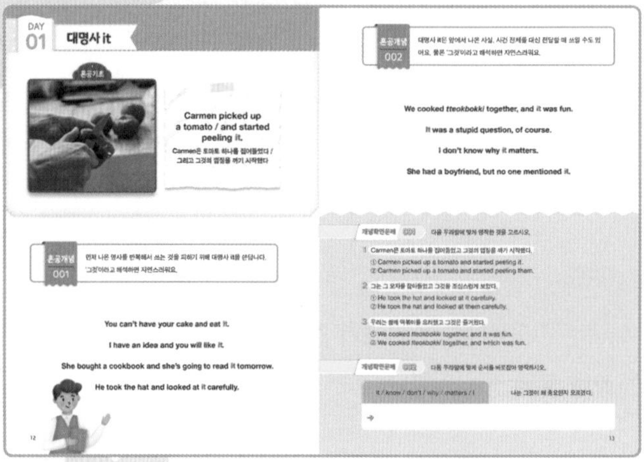

DAY 01 대명사 it

Carmen picked up a tomato / and started peeling it.

Carmen은 토마토 하나를 집어들었다 / 그리고 그것의 껍질을 까기 시작했다

혼공개념 001

You can't have your cake and eat it.

I have an idea and you will like it.

She bought a cookbook and she's going to read it tomorrow.

He took the hat and looked at it carefully.

12

혼공개념 002

We cooked *tteokbokki* together, and it was fun.

It was a stupid question, of course.

I don't know why it matters.

She had a boyfriend, but no one mentioned it.

1 ① Carmen picked up a tomato and started peeling it.
② Carmen picked up a tomato and started peeling them.

2 ① He took the hat and looked at it carefully.
② He took the hat and looked at them carefully.

3 ① We cooked *tteokbokki* together, and it was fun.
② We cooked *tteokbokki* together, and which was fun.

it / know / don't / why / matters / I

→

13

최소의 개념으로 핵심 문장을 공부해요. 적절한 분량의 예문으로 개념을 익히고, 간단한 간접 영작을 통해 적용을 해본답니다. 할 수 있다는 자신감이 생길 거예요.

2 혼공연습

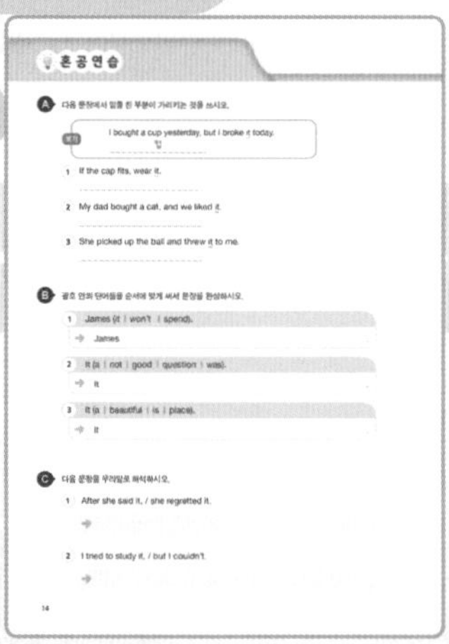

혼공연습

A

I bought a cup yesterday, but I broke it today.

1 If the cap fits, wear it.

2 My dad bought a cat, and we liked it.

3 She picked up the ball and threw it to me.

B

1 James (it | won't | spend).
→ James

2 It (a | not | good | question | was).
→ It

3 It (a | beautiful | is | place).
→ It

C

1 After she said it, / she regretted it.
→

2 I tried to study it, / but I couldn't.
→

14

간단한 문항을 풀면서 개념을 반복 적용하고 서서히 확장시켜 나갑니다. 우리말 해석부터 힌트가 주어진 쉬운 영작까지 어렵지 않게 할 수 있어요.

3 혼공완성

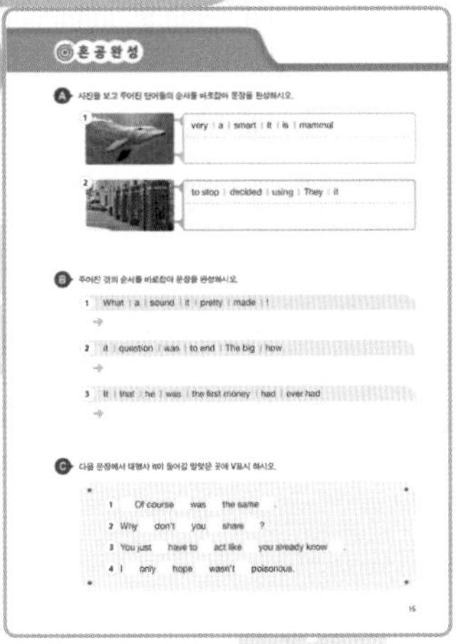
혼공완성

A
1 very | a | smart | it | is | mammal
2 to stop | decided | using | They | it

B
1 What | a | sound | it | pretty | made | !
2 it | question | was | to end | The big | how
3 it | that | he | was | the first money | had | ever had

C
1 Of course was the same
2 Why don't you share ?
3 You just have to act like you already know
4 I only hope wasn't poisonous.

실제 생활과 관련된 사진을 보면서 영작을 한 다음, 힌트가 최소화 된 영작을 하면서 가장 난도가 높은 문제까지 순서대로 다뤄요. 마지막으로, 개념이 적용된 다양한 유형의 문항을 다루면서 실전 감각을 끌어올려요.

4 혼공복습

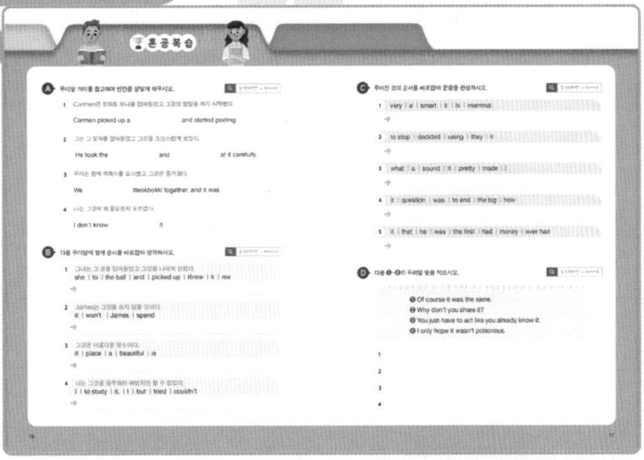
혼공복습

A
1 Carmen picked up a and started peeling
2 He took the and at it carefully.
3 We tteokbokki together, and it was
4 I don't know it

B
1 she | to | the ball | and | picked up | threw | it | me
2 it | won't | James | spend
3 it | place | a | beautiful | is
4 I | to study | it, | I | but | tried | couldn't

C
1 very | a | smart | it | is | mammal
2 to stop | decided | using | they | it
3 what | a | sound | it | pretty | made | !
4 it | question | was | to end | the big | how
5 it | that | he | was | the first | had | money | ever had

D
❶ Of course it was the same.
❷ Why don't you share it?
❸ You just have to act like you already know it.
❹ I only hope it wasn't poisonous.

하나의 Day 학습을 효과적으로 마무리 할 수 있는 복습 코너예요. 가장 쉬운 A문항부터, 우리말 의미에 맞게 문장이나 어구를 쓰는 좀 더 어려운 B문항까지 순서대로 제공해요. 이후 더 어려운 C문항의 영작, 마지막 우리말 의미 파악 D문항 까지 체계적으로 풀고 나면 완전학습을 할 수 있어요.

목차

〈혼공기초구문 레벨 3〉

하루 30~40분, 20일만에 기초구문 **완전정복**하기!

하루 30~40분 집중 학습으로 20일 동안 중학영어 과정에서 알아야 할 기초 구문을 마스터할 수 있는 Study Plan입니다. 학습 후 ◯에 V 표시 하세요.

◯ Day 01	◯ Day 02	◯ Day 03	◯ Day 04	◯ Day 05
대명사 it	강조구문의 it	비인칭 주어 it	시간/조건의 접속사	원인/결과/목적의 접속사
◯ Day 06	◯ Day 07	◯ Day 08	◯ Day 09	◯ Day 10
대조의 접속사	가정법 과거	가정법 과거완료	if가 생략된 가정법	혼합가정법
◯ Day 11	◯ Day 12	◯ Day 13	◯ Day 14	◯ Day 15
wish 가정법	as if 가정법	부정구문	도치구문	삽입/동격구문
◯ Day 16	◯ Day 17	◯ Day 18	◯ Day 19	◯ Day 20
생략/공통구문	실전구문독해 Ⅰ	실전구문독해 Ⅱ	실전구문독해 Ⅲ	실전구문독해 Ⅳ

★ 무료 유튜브 강의와 함께 학습하면 훨씬 더 효율적입니다. 아래의 QR코드를 찍어 보세요!

★ 더 많은 강의는 혼공마켓 클래스룸 (https://hongong.co.kr/classroom)에서 보실 수 있습니다.

혼공 N 혼공마켓

Part 1

it의 확장
다양한 it

- Day 01 **Carmen picked up a tomato and started peeling it.**
- Day 02 **It is the technology that helps people to work better.**
- Day 03 **It's four miles from here to the store.**

DAY 01

대명사 it

혼공기초

Carmen picked up a tomato / and started peeling it.

Carmen은 토마토 하나를 집어들었다 / 그리고 그것의 껍질을 까기 시작했다

혼공개념 001

먼저 나온 명사를 반복해서 쓰는 것을 피하기 위해 대명사 **it**을 쓴답니다. '그것'이라고 해석하면 자연스러워요.

You can't have your cake and eat it.

I have an idea and you will like it.

She bought a cookbook and she's going to read it tomorrow.

He took the hat and looked at it carefully.

혼공개념 002

대명사 **it**은 앞에서 나온 사실, 사건 전체를 대신 전달할 때 쓰일 수도 있어요. 물론 '그것'이라고 해석하면 자연스러워요.

We cooked *tteokbokki* together, and it was fun.

It was a stupid question, of course.

I don't know why it matters.

She had a boyfriend, but no one mentioned it.

개념확인문제 001 다음 우리말에 맞게 영작한 것을 고르시오.

1 Carmen은 토마토 하나를 집어들었고 그것의 껍질을 까기 시작했다.

① Carmen picked up a tomato and started peeling it.
② Carmen picked up a tomato and started peeling them.

2 그는 그 모자를 잡아들었고 그것을 조심스럽게 보았다.

① He took the hat and looked at it carefully.
② He took the hat and looked at them carefully.

3 우리는 함께 떡볶이를 요리했고 그것은 즐거웠다.

① We cooked *tteokbokki* together, and it was fun.
② We cooked *tteokbokki* together, and which was fun.

개념확인문제 002 다음 우리말에 맞게 순서를 바로잡아 영작하시오.

it / know / don't / why / matters / I

나는 그것이 왜 중요한지 모르겠다.

➜

혼공연습

A 다음 문장에서 밑줄 친 부분이 가리키는 것을 쓰시오.

보기 I bought a cup yesterday, but I broke <u>it</u> today.
컵

1 If the cap fits, wear <u>it</u>.

____

2 My dad bought a cat, and we liked <u>it</u>.

____

3 She picked up the ball and threw <u>it</u> to me.

____

B 괄호 안의 단어들을 순서에 맞게 써서 문장을 완성하시오.

1 James (it | won't | spend).
→ James ______________________ .

2 It (a | not | good | question | was).
→ It ______________________ .

3 It (a | beautiful | is | place).
→ It ______________________ .

C 다음 문장을 우리말로 해석하시오.

1 After she said it, / she regretted it.
→

2 I tried to study it, / but I couldn't.
→

혼공완성

A 사진을 보고 주어진 단어들의 순서를 바로잡아 문장을 완성하시오.

1

very | a | smart | It | is | mammal

2

to stop | decided | using | They | it

B 주어진 것의 순서를 바로잡아 문장을 완성하시오.

1 What | a | sound | it | pretty | made | !

→

2 it | question | was | to end | The big | how

→

3 It | that | he | was | the first money | had | ever had

→

C 다음 문장에서 대명사 it이 들어갈 알맞은 곳에 V표시 하시오.

1 Of course was the same .

2 Why don't you share ?

3 You just have to act like you already know .

4 I only hope wasn't poisonous.

혼공복습

A 우리말 의미를 참고하여 빈칸을 알맞게 채우시오.

잘 모르겠다면 ⋯› 13페이지로

1. Carmen은 토마토 하나를 집어들었고 그것의 껍질을 까기 시작했다.

   Carmen picked up a ____________ and started peeling ____________.

2. 그는 그 모자를 잡아들었고 그것을 조심스럽게 보았다.

   He took the ____________ and ____________ at it carefully.

3. 우리는 함께 떡볶이를 요리했고 그것은 즐거웠다.

   We ____________ *tteokbokki* together, and it was ____________.

4. 나는 그것이 왜 중요한지 모르겠다.

   I don't know ____________ it ____________.

B 다음 우리말에 맞게 순서를 바로잡아 영작하시오.

잘 모르겠다면 ⋯› 14페이지로

1. 그녀는 그 공을 집어들었고 그것을 나에게 던졌다.
   she | to | the ball | and | picked up | threw | it | me

   ➜

2. James는 그것을 쓰지 않을 것이다.
   it | won't | James | spend

   ➜

3. 그것은 아름다운 장소이다.
   it | place | a | beautiful | is

   ➜

4. 나는 그것을 공부하려 애썼지만 할 수 없었다.
   I | to study | it, | I | but | tried | couldn't

   ➜

C 주어진 것의 순서를 바로잡아 문장을 완성하시오.

잘 모르겠다면 ..., 15페이지로

1 very | a | smart | it | is | mammal

→

2 to stop | decided | using | they | it

→

3 what | a | sound | it | pretty | made | !

→

4 it | question | was | to end | the big | how

→

5 it | that | he | was | the first | had | money | ever had

→

D 다음 ❶~❹의 우리말 뜻을 적으시오.

잘 모르겠다면 ..., 15페이지로

❶ Of course it was the same.
❷ Why don't you share it?
❸ You just have to act like you already know it.
❹ I only hope it wasn't poisonous.

1

2

3

4

DAY 02 강조구문의 it

혼공기초

It is the technology / that helps people to work better.

그것은 바로 그 기술이다 /
사람들이 더 잘 일하도록 돕는 것은

혼공개념 001

강조 하고 싶은 내용을 **it**과 **that** 사이에 넣어서 표현하는 것을 강조구문이라고 해요. '바로 ~ 이다 **that** ~ 하는 것은'이라고 해석하면 자연스러워요.

It is the new Super Mario game that I want to buy.

It was in the early morning that Kevin was walking around at school.

It was five years ago that I participated in the Terry Fox Run.

It was to make money that I was working so hard.

혼공개념 002

강조하고 싶은 대상이 사물, 사람, 시간, 장소면 **that** 대신 각각 **which, who(m), when, where**을 쓸 수 있어요.

It was *bibimbap* which my mom made for us.

It was Jason who stopped laughing and said "It's dangerous".

It was yesterday when he came back home.

It is at the stadium where the concert will take place.

개념확인문제 001 다음 우리말에 맞게 영작한 것을 고르시오.

1 내가 사고 싶은 것은 바로 뉴 슈퍼 마리오 게임이다.

① It is the new Super Mario game who I want to buy.
② It is the new Super Mario game that I want to buy.

2 내가 테리 팍스 런에 참가했던 것은 바로 5년 전이었다.

① It was five years ago that I participated in the Terry Fox Run.
② It was five years ago which I participated in the Terry Fox Run.

3 웃음을 멈추고 "그것은 위험해."라고 말했던 사람은 바로 Jason이었다.

① It was Jason who stopped laughing and said "It's dangerous".
② It was Jason which stopped laughing and said "It's dangerous".

개념확인문제 002 다음 우리말에 맞게 순서를 바로잡아 영작하시오.

the concert / is / will / at the stadium / where / It / take place	그 콘서트가 열릴 것은 바로 그 경기장에서 이다.

➜

혼공연습

A 다음 문장에서 밑줄 친 부분을 알맞게 해석하시오.

보기 It was under the bridge where the police officer found a dog.
경찰관이 개를 발견했던 곳은

1 It was several years ago that Myeongdong was famous in Korea.

____

2 It was his neighbor who she saw at the door.

____

3 It was his powerful light that he was very proud of.

____

B 괄호 안의 단어들을 순서에 맞게 써서 문장을 완성하시오.

1 It was his hard work (him | win | that | helped | a competition).

➜

2 It was him (tried to | who | huge mountains | climb | these).

➜

3 It is Dr. Smith (went | many people | to Africa | to take care of | who).

➜

C 다음 문장을 우리말로 해석하시오.

1 It is him / whom I would like to tell you about.

➜

2 It is the cooking class / that Tommy wants to join.

➜

혼공완성

A 사진을 보고 의미에 맞게 괄호 안의 것을 순서대로 쓰시오.

1 

It is the newspaper (every day | Tom | that | reads).

2 

It was my family (with | camping | I | went | who).

B 괄호 안의 단어들을 순서에 맞게 써서 문장을 완성하시오.

1 It is the safety (have to | that | you | rules | follow).

→

2 It is the K-pop (in | that | I'm | song | interested).

→

3 It is the (have to | classroom | we | that | clean up).

→

C 다음 문장에서 주어진 단어가 들어갈 알맞은 곳에 V표시 하시오.

1 It is before doing the laundry people should check the amount of clothes . (when)

2 It was Lena liked looking at the stars in the sky. (who)

3 It is snow these beautiful art pieces are made of . (which)

4 It is Koreans make food and share it with other people . (that)

혼공복습

A 우리말 의미를 참고하여 빈칸을 알맞게 채우시오.

잘 모르겠다면 ···› 19페이지로

1 내가 사고 싶은 것은 바로 뉴 슈퍼 마리오 게임이다.

It is the new Super Mario __________ that I want to __________.

2 내가 테리 팍스 런에 참가했던 것은 바로 5년 전이었다.

It was five __________ ago that I __________ in the Terry Fox Run.

3 웃음을 멈추고 "그것은 위험해."라고 말했던 사람은 바로 Jason이었다.

It was Jason who __________ laughing and __________ "It's dangerous".

4 그 콘서트가 열릴 것은 바로 그 경기장에서 이다.

It is at the __________ where the concert will __________ place.

B 다음 우리말에 맞게 순서를 바로잡아 영작하시오.

잘 모르겠다면 ···› 20페이지로

1 경찰관이 개를 발견했던 곳은 바로 그 다리 아래였다.
It was under the bridge (the police officer | found | where | a dog).

➜

2 그가 대회에서 우승하도록 도와준 것은 바로 그의 근면이었다.
It was his hard work (him | win | that | helped | a competition).

➜

3 많은 사람들을 돌보기 위해 아프리카로 간 사람은 바로 Smith 박사였다.
It is Dr. Smith (went | many people | to Africa | to take care of | who).

➜

4 Tommy가 참가하고 싶은 것은 바로 그 요리 수업이다.
It is the cooking class (that | wants | Tommy | to join).

➜

C 괄호 안의 단어들을 순서에 맞게 써서 문장을 완성하시오.

잘 모르겠다면 ···› 21페이지로

1 It is the newspaper (every day | Tom | that | reads).

➜

2 It was my family (with | camping | I | went | who).

➜

3 It is the safety (have to | that | you | rules | follow).

➜

4 It is the K-pop (in | that | I'm | song | interested).

➜

5 It is the (have to | classroom | we | that | clean up).

➜

D 다음 ❶~❹의 우리말 뜻을 적으시오.

잘 모르겠다면 ···› 21페이지로

❶ It is before doing the laundry when people should check the amount of clothes.
❷ It was Lena who liked looking at the stars in the sky.
❸ It is snow which these beautiful art pieces are made of.
❹ It is Koreans that make food and share it with other people.

1

2

3

4

DAY 03

비인칭 주어 it

혼공기초

It's four miles / from here to the store.

4마일이다 / 여기서 가게까지는

혼공개념 001

it이 '그것'이라는 의미 없이 일반적인 내용을 나타내면서 주어 자리에 오는 것을 비인칭주어라고 해요. 날씨, 시각, 요일, 계절에 주로 쓰이며 **it**은 굳이 해석하지 않고 '~이다'라고 해석하면 자연스러워요.

It's cold outside.

It was almost three o'clock in the afternoon.

It's Monday today, isn't it?

It's summer in Korea.

혼공개념 002

비인칭주어 **it**이 거리, 명암을 표현할 때도 쓰여요. 거리는 형용사 **far** 또는 다양한 거리 단위가 쓰이고, 명암은 날이 어두워지거나 밝아질 때 쓰여요. 주로 **dark**, **bright**와 같은 형용사와 같이 쓰인답니다.

How far is it to the post office?

It is 500 meters from the post office to the bus stop.

It's getting dark.

It's too bright, so I can't see anything!

개념확인문제 001 다음 우리말에 맞게 영작한 것을 고르시오.

1 여기서 가게까지는 4마일이다.

① It's four miles from here to the store.
② It has four miles from here to the store.

2 거의 오후 세 시 정각이었다.

① It is almost three o'clock in the afternoon.
② It was almost three o'clock in the afternoon.

3 우체국까지 얼마나 머니?

① How far it is to the post office?
② How far is it to the post office?

개념확인문제 002 다음 우리말에 맞게 순서를 바로잡아 영작하시오.

It's / can't / see / so / too / I / anything / bright

너무나 밝아서 나는 아무것도 볼 수가 없다.

➜

혼공연습

A 다음 문장에서 밑줄 친 it이 날씨, 시각, 요일, 거리, 명암 중에 나타내는 것을 쓰시오.

보기 It's probably Wednesday.
요일

1 It's windy.

____

2 It was Monday yesterday.

____

3 If it's too far, let's just take a taxi.

____

B 괄호 안의 단어들을 순서에 맞게 써서 문장을 완성하시오.

1 It (till | snows | February).

→ It ______________ .

2 It (in | rains | Vancouver | a lot).

→ It ______________ .

3 Is (from | far | it | here)?

→ Is ______________ ?

C 다음 문장을 우리말로 해석하시오.

1 It may rain, / but I will go out anyhow.

→

2 It might be cloudy, / but that's okay.

→

혼공완성

A 사진을 보고 주어진 단어들의 순서를 바로잡아 문장을 완성하시오.

1 

in | is | her | It | dark | room

2 

was | It | yesterday | freezing

B 주어진 단어들의 순서를 바로잡아 문장을 완성하시오.

1 an hour | on foot | It | to get | takes | there

→

2 three hours | takes | from Busan | usually | to Seoul | It

→

3 about | It | by train | takes | five hours

→

C 다음 문장에서 밑줄 친 it의 성격이 다른 하나를 골라 □에 V표시 하시오.

1 What day is it today? □

2 It was so hot in Atlanta. □

3 It's going to rain. □

4 It's sunny today. □

혼공복습

A 우리말 의미를 참고하여 빈칸을 알맞게 채우시오.

잘 모르겠다면 ···› 25페이지로

1 여기서 가게까지는 4마일이다.

It's ________ miles from ________ to the store.

2 거의 오후 세 시 정각이었다.

It was ________ three o'clock in the ________.

3 우체국까지 얼마나 머니?

How ________ is ________ to the post office?

4 너무나 밝아서 나는 아무것도 볼 수가 없다.

It's too ________ so I can't ________ anything.

B 다음 우리말에 맞게 순서를 바로잡아 영작하시오.

잘 모르겠다면 ···› 26페이지로

1 어제는 월요일이었다.
was | it | yesterday | Monday

➜

2 Vancouver에는 비가 많이 온다.
in | rains | it | Vancouver | a lot

➜

3 그곳은 여기서 머니?
from | far | it | is | here | ?

➜

4 날씨가 흐릴지도 모르지만, 괜찮아.
but | might | cloudy, | that's | it | be | okay

➜

C 주어진 단어들의 순서를 바로잡아 문장을 완성하시오.

잘 모르겠다면 ··· 27페이지로

1 in | is | her | it | dark | room

→

2 was | it | yesterday | freezing

→

3 an hour | on foot | it | to get | takes | there

→

4 three hours | takes | from Busan | usually | to Seoul | it

→

5 about | it | by train | takes | five hours

→

D 다음 ❶~❹의 우리말 뜻을 적으시오.

잘 모르겠다면 ··· 27페이지로

❶ What day is it today?
❷ It was so hot in Atlanta.
❸ It's going to rain.
❹ It's sunny today.

1

2

3

4

Part 2

내용의 확장 접속사

- **Day 04** He became interested in volcanoes while he was in high school.
- **Day 05** They were angry because their plans had been discovered.
- **Day 06** Though he was wearing new shoes, he couldn't run fast.

DAY 04

시간/조건의 접속사

혼공기초

He became interested in volcanoes / while he was in high school.

그는 화산에 관심이 생겼다 / 그가 고등학교에 있는 동안

혼공개념 001

시간을 나타내는 접속사에는 다음과 같은 것들이 있어요. **when**(~할 때), **while**(~하는 동안에), **before**(~하기 전에), **after**(~한 후에), **since**(~이후로), **as**(~할 때, ~하면서, ~함에 따라), **until**(~까지), **as soon as**(~하자마자)를 기억하세요.

It must have happened while I was sleeping.

You've been quiet for weeks since we left Texas.

As we get older, we get weaker.

The dogs ran off as soon as we appeared.

혼공개념 002

조건을 나타내는 접속사에는 다음과 같은 것들이 있어요. **if**(만약 ~라면), **unless**(만약 ~가 아니라면), **as long as**(~하는 한)가 대표적인 표현이니 꼭 알아두세요. 특히 **unless**는 **if ~ not**의 의미이기 때문에 그 속에 담긴 부정의 해석에 주의해야 해요.

If you change your mind, just call me.

They wouldn't be there unless something terrible happened.

I don't want you to give that number to anyone unless it's an emergency.

I don't care as long as you love me.

개념확인문제 001 다음 우리말에 맞게 영작한 것을 고르시오.

1 그는 그가 고등학교에 있는 동안 화산에 관심이 생겼다.

① He became interested in volcanoes since he was in high school.
② He became interested in volcanoes while he was in high school.

2 그것은 내가 자고 있는 동안에 일어났던 것이 틀림없다.

① It must have happened while I was sleeping.
② It must have happened as soon as I was sleeping.

3 어떤 끔찍한 일이 일어나지 않는다면 그들은 거기에 있지 않을 것이다.

① They wouldn't be there if something terrible happened.
② They wouldn't be there unless something terrible happened.

개념확인문제 002 다음 우리말에 맞게 순서를 바로잡아 영작하시오.

you / don't / love / care / as long as / me / I	당신이 나를 사랑하는 한 나는 상관하지 않는다.

➜

혼공연습

A 다음 문장에서 밑줄 친 부분을 알맞게 해석하시오.

보기
He had been there when she needed him.
그녀가 그를 필요로 했을 때

1 He had climbed many trees when he was a boy.

2 After I had dinner, I went to Cheonggyecheon for a walk.

3 I can't forget it as long as I live.

B 괄호 안의 단어들을 의미에 맞게 순서대로 쓰시오.

1 (cannot | If | you | bite), never show your teeth.
➜

2 (he | When | answered), his voice was quiet.
➜

3 It has been a long time (met | we | since).
➜

C 다음 문장을 우리말로 해석하시오.

1 After he left, / she picked up one of the suitcases and / placed it on the bed.
➜

2 People swept the streets at night / until a machine replaced them.
➜

혼공완성

A 사진을 보고 의미에 맞게 괄호 안의 것을 순서대로 쓰시오.

1

He slept (everybody | the morning | woke up | in | until).

2

(as | the door | I | As | soon | opened), I smelled the aroma of fresh coffee.

B 괄호 안의 단어들을 순서에 맞게 써서 문장을 완성하시오.

1 I want to follow them (are | they | when | going | out).

➜

2 Let's wait (bell | until | rings | the school).

➜

3 It lasted for over 900 years (the Romans | closed | it | was | by | until).

➜

C if 또는 unless를 활용하여 다음 ①과 ②, ③과 ④를 각각 연결하시오.

① Call me.
② It's a real emergency.
③ My baby sister never cries.
④ She is hungry.

1 + 2 ______________________

3 + 4 ______________________

혼공복습

A 우리말 의미를 참고하여 빈칸을 알맞게 채우시오.

잘 모르겠다면 ···› 33페이지로

1 그는 그가 고등학교에 있는 동안 화산에 관심이 생겼다.

He became interested in ________ he was in high school.

2 그것은 내가 자고 있는 동안에 일어났던 것이 틀림없다.

It ________ have happened ________ I was sleeping.

3 어떤 끔찍한 일이 일어나지 않는다면 그들은 거기에 있지 않을 것이다.

They wouldn't be there ________ something ________ happened.

4 당신이 나를 사랑하는 한 나는 상관하지 않는다.

I don't ________ as ________ as you love me.

B 다음 우리말에 맞게 순서를 바로잡아 영작하시오.

잘 모르겠다면 ···› 34페이지로

1 내가 살아있는 한 나는 그것을 잊을 수 없다.
I can't forget it (long | as | I | as | live).

➜

2 만약 네가 물 수 없다면, 절대 너의 이빨을 드러내지 마라.
(cannot | if | you | bite), never show your teeth.

➜

3 우리가 만난 이후로 오랜만이다.
It has been a long time (met | we | since).

➜

4 기계가 그들을 대체할 때까지 사람들은 밤에 거리를 쓸었다.
People swept the streets at night (a machine | until | replaced | them).

➜

C 괄호 안의 단어들을 의미에 맞게 순서대로 쓰시오.

잘 모르겠다면 ··· 35페이지로

1 He slept (everybody | the morning | woke up | in | until).

➜

2 (as | the door | I | as | soon | opened), I smelled the aroma of fresh coffee.

➜

3 I want to follow them (are | they | when | going | out).

➜

4 Let's wait (bell | until | rings | the school).

➜

5 It lasted for over 900 years (the Romans | closed | it | was | by | until).

➜

D 다음 ❶~❹의 우리말 뜻을 적으시오.

잘 모르겠다면 ··· 35페이지로

❶ Call me.
❷ It's a real emergency.
❷ My baby sister never cries.
❹ She is hungry.

1

2

3

4

DAY 05

원인/결과/목적의 접속사

혼공기초

They were angry / because their plans had been discovered.

그들은 화가 났다 / 그들의 계획이 발견되었기 때문에

혼공개념 001

because, **as**, **since** 셋 다 '~이기 때문에'로 원인을 나타내는 접속사랍니다. 물론 **as**와 **since**는 문맥에 따라 다른 뜻으로 쓰일 수도 있으니 주의하세요.

Is it because winning the award gives them more confidence?

I felt sorry for them as they cried a lot.

First of all, I married Alex as I love him.

I said it would be dangerous since the enemy was coming.

혼공개념 002

다음과 같은 표현은 목적/결과를 나타내는 부사절을 이끌기 때문에 꼭 알아두세요. 특히 **so that**은 앞에 콤마가 있고 없고에 따라 의미가 다르기 때문에 주의해야 해요.

so that(~하기 위해서)

, so that(그래서)

so 형용사/**such** 명사 + **that**(아주 ~ 해서 그 결과 ~하다)

I organized my desk so that I could find things easily.

They were starved, so (that) they ate an entire cake.

It was so dark that I couldn't see his expression.

Mr. Kim is such a genius that he can answer all the questions.

개념확인문제 001 다음 우리말에 맞게 영작한 것을 고르시오.

1 그들은 그들의 계획이 발견되었기 때문에 화가 났다.

① They were angry so that their plans had been discovered.
② They were angry because their plans had been discovered.

2 그들이 많이 울었기 때문에 나는 그들에게 미안하다.

① I am sorry for them as they cried a lot.
② I am sorry for them so they cried a lot.

3 내가 물건들을 쉽게 찾을 수 있도록 나는 책상을 정리했다.

① I organized my desk so that I could find things easily.
② I organized my desk such that I could find things easily.

개념확인문제 002 다음 우리말에 맞게 순서를 바로잡아 영작하시오.

dark / that / I / It / couldn't / was / see / his / expression / so

너무나 어두워서 나는 그의 표현을 볼 수 없었다.

➜

혼공연습

A 다음 문장에서 밑줄 친 부분을 알맞게 해석하시오.

보기
He is delighted because I am here.
내가 여기에 있기 때문에

1 We have to work as we buy many products.

2 It was so fast that she didn't have time to think.

3 We do what we have to do so that we can do what we want to do.

B 괄호 안의 단어들을 순서에 맞게 써서 문장을 완성하시오.

1 I was so excited (I | wait | couldn't | until | that | midnight).
➜

2 It was such bad weather (we | that | go | couldn't | out).
➜

3 Put the food on the table (can | so | that | everyone | eat).
➜

C 다음 문장을 우리말로 해석하시오.

1 Since this is the only power they know, / it is the only power they respect.
➜

2 Thousands of people research diseases / because they want to cure them.
➜

혼공완성

A 사진을 보고 주어진 단어들의 순서를 바로잡아 문장을 완성하시오.

1 

The cake was (so | everyone | delicious | liked | that | it).

2 

It was (so | for dinner | much that | could | eat | people).

B 주어진 단어들의 순서를 바로잡아 문장을 완성하시오.

1 I love to go to school (I | to | like | see | my | because | friends).

→

2 Her stride was (that | difficult | to catch | it | was | so | long | her).

→

3 I went there (was | booking | accessible | the palace | since | without).

→

C ❶~❹의 괄호 안에서 어법상 알맞은 것을 골라 아래에 쓰시오.

❶ I was [so / such] worried that I couldn't think of anything.
❷ We were having [so / such] a good time that we decided to stay longer.
❸ It's [so / such] late that people are starting to give up.
❹ His plan was [so / such] a success that even his competitors praised him.

1 ________ 2 ________ 3 ________ 4 ________

혼공복습

A 우리말 의미를 참고하여 빈칸을 알맞게 채우시오.

잘 모르겠다면 ···› 39페이지로

1. 그들은 그들의 계획이 발견되었기 때문에 화가 났다.

   They were ________ because their plans had been ________.

2. 그들이 많이 울었기 때문에 나는 그들에게 미안하다.

   I am ________ for them as they ________ a lot.

3. 내가 물건들을 쉽게 찾을 수 있도록 나는 책상을 정리했다.

   I ________ my desk so that I could ________ things easily.

4. 너무나 어두워서 나는 그의 표현을 볼 수 없었다.

   It was so ________ that I couldn't see his ________.

B 다음 우리말에 맞게 순서를 바로잡아 영작하시오.

잘 모르겠다면 ···› 40페이지로

1. 그것은 너무나 빨라서 그녀는 생각할 시간이 없었다.
   It was so fast (she | to think | didn't | that | have | time).

   ➜

2. 나는 너무 신나서 한밤중까지 기다릴 수 없었다.
   I was so excited (I | wait | couldn't | until | that | midnight).

   ➜

3. 너무나 날씨가 나빠서 우리는 밖에 나갈 수 없었다.
   It was such bad weather (we | that | go | couldn't | out).

   ➜

4. 모든 사람들이 먹을 수 있도록 음식을 탁자 위에 두어라.
   Put the food on the table (can | so | that | everyone | eat).

   ➜

C 주어진 단어들의 순서를 바로잡아 문장을 완성하시오.

잘 모르겠다면 ···› 41페이지로

1 The cake was (so | everyone | delicious | liked | that | it).

➔

2 It was (so | for dinner | much that | could | eat | people).

➔

3 I love to go to school (I | to | like | see | my | because | friends).

➔

4 Her stride was (that | difficult | to catch | it | was | so | long | her).

➔

5 I went there (was | booking | accessible | the palace | since | without).

➔

D 다음 ❶~❹의 우리말 뜻을 적으시오.

잘 모르겠다면 ···› 41페이지로

❶ I was so worried that I couldn't think of anything.
❷ We were having such a good time that we decided to stay longer.
❸ It's so late that people are starting to give up.
❹ His plan was such a success that even his competitors praised him.

1

2

3

4

DAY 06

대조의 접속사

혼공기초

Though he was wearing new shoes, / he couldn't run fast.

그가 새 신발을 신고 있었음에도 불구하고, / 그는 빨리 달릴 수 없었다

혼공개념 001

대조를 나타내는 접속사에는 다음과 같은 것들이 있어요. **though**(~에도 불구하고), **although**(~에도 불구하고), **while**(~인 반면에)을 기억하세요. 특히 **while**은 문맥에 따라 '~동안에'로도 해석되기 때문에 주의해야 해요.

Though she's almost 80, she still studies several languages.

Although she is very young, she is very independent.

While it is a small town, there are several local restaurants available.

Make hay while the sun shines.

혼공개념 002

even though와 **even if**는 **though**, **if**보다 강조된 의미로 종종 쓰여요. 각각 '심지어 ~에도 불구하고', '심지어 ~일지라도'라는 해석하며, '**even though** + 일어난 일 또는 사실', '**even if** + 가정'을 사용한답니다.

Even though we are apart, you are in my heart.

She never took a taxi, even though she could afford to.

Even if they are rich, they will live simply.

I will make this radio work even if I have to stay up all night.

개념확인문제 001 다음 우리말에 맞게 영작한 것을 고르시오.

1 그가 새 신발을 신고 있었음에도 불구하고, 그는 빨리 달릴 수 없었다.

① Even if he was wearing new shoes, he couldn't run fast.
② Though he was wearing new shoes, he couldn't run fast.

2 그녀가 거의 80살임에도 불구하고, 여전히 여러 개의 언어를 공부한다.

① Though she's almost 80, she still studies several languages.
② Because she's almost 80, she still studies several languages.

3 심지어 여력이 있었음에도 불구하고, 그녀는 절대 택시를 타지 않았다.

① She never took a taxi, even if she could afford to.
② She never took a taxi, even though she could afford to.

개념확인문제 002 다음 우리말에 맞게 순서를 바로잡아 영작하시오.

they / they / live / are / simply / rich, / will / Even if

심지어 그들이 부유할 지라도, 그들은 단순하게 살 것이다.

➜

혼공연습

A 다음 문장에서 밑줄 친 부분을 알맞게 해석하시오.

보기 He will make this computer work even if he has to stay up all night.
심지어 그가 밤을 세워야 할지라도

1 The phone woke me up, even though it wasn't very loud.

2 He wore jeans to the meeting, while others wore formal clothes.

3 My house was not empty although I was gone.

B 괄호 안의 단어들을 의미에 맞게 순서대로 쓰시오.

1 (my | could | I | raise | Although | not | arms), I kept working.
➜

2 He spoke very fast (was | talking | he | to | though | his grandparents).
➜

3 Speak your mind, (your | even | if | voice | shakes).
➜

C 다음 문장을 우리말로 해석하시오.

1 We are better off than we were, / even though nothing has been created.
➜

2 They only speak Spanish, / while we can speak several languages.
➜

혼공완성

A 사진을 보고 의미에 맞게 괄호 안의 것을 순서대로 쓰시오.

1 

She hated this house (it | was | though | beautiful).

2 

(was | though | getting | Even | he | angry), his voice remained calm.

B 괄호 안의 단어들을 의미에 맞게 순서대로 쓰시오.

1 (her | Though | color | was red | favorite), she chose the blue dress.

→

2 They stay awake at night (researchers | in | work | while | the daytime).

→

3 (discussed | Even | was | not | though | the issue), he couldn't stop thinking about it.

→

C ❶~❹의 괄호 안에서 의미상 알맞은 것을 골라 아래에 쓰시오.

❶ Even [if / though] I had an hour, I wouldn't go out shopping.
❷ She smiled at them even [if / though] they had betrayed her.
❸ Even [if / though] he loses his job, he'll continue his career.
❹ I've caught a cold even [if / though] I wore several layers of clothes.

1 ________ 2 ________ 3 ________ 4 ________

혼공복습

A 우리말 의미를 참고하여 빈칸을 알맞게 채우시오.

잘 모르겠다면 ···› 45페이지로

1 그가 새 신발을 신고 있었음에도 불구하고, 그는 빨리 달릴 수 없었다.

_______ he was _______ new shoes, he couldn't run fast.

2 그녀가 거의 80살임에도 불구하고, 여전히 여러 개의 언어를 공부한다.

Though she's almost 80, she still _______ several _______.

3 심지어 여력이 있었음에도 불구하고, 그녀는 절대 택시를 타지 않았다.

She never _______ a taxi, even though she could _______ to.

4 심지어 그들이 부유할 지라도, 그들은 단순하게 살 것이다.

Even _______ they are rich, they will _______ simply.

B 다음 우리말에 맞게 순서를 바로잡아 영작하시오.

잘 모르겠다면 ···› 46페이지로

1 그가 회의에 청바지를 입고 온 반면, 다른 사람들은 정장을 입었다.
He wore jeans to the meeting, (others | while | formal | wore | clothes).

→

2 나는 내 팔을 들어올릴 수 없었음에도 불구하고, 계속 일을 했다.
(my | could | I | raise | although | not | arms), I kept working.

→

3 그는 그의 조부모님께 말하는 중이었음에도 불구하고, 아주 빨리 말했다.
He spoke very fast (was | talking | he | to | though | his grandparents).

→

4 그들이 단지 스페인어만 하는 반면, 우리는 여러 개의 언어를 할 수 있다.
They only speak Spanish, (while | several languages | can | we | speak).

→

C 괄호 안의 단어들을 의미에 맞게 순서대로 쓰시오.

잘 모르겠다면 ···› 47페이지로

1 She hated this house (it | was | though | beautiful).

➜

2 (was | though | getting | even | he | angry), his voice remained calm.

➜

3 (her | though | color | was red | favorite), she chose the blue dress.

➜

4 They stay awake at night (researchers | in | work | while | the daytime).

➜

5 (discussed | even | was | not | though | the issue), he couldn't stop thinking about it.

➜

D 다음 ❶~❹의 우리말 뜻을 적으시오.

잘 모르겠다면 ···› 47페이지로

❶ Even if I had an hour, I wouldn't go out shopping.
❷ She smiled at them even though they had betrayed her.
❸ Even if he loses his job, he'll continue his career.
❹ I've caught a cold even though I wore several layers of clothes.

1

2

3

4

Part 3

생각의 확장 가정법

- **Day 07** If he knew how to read, he could enjoy the book.
- **Day 08** If I had lost the ring, he would have really blamed me.
- **Day 09** Provided I went to school, I could study with my friends.
- **Day 10** If he hadn't got tickets, we would never be here now.
- **Day 11** I wish I were taller than John.
- **Day 12** He acts as if he were the owner of the house.

DAY 07

가정법 과거

혼공기초

If he knew how to read, / he could enjoy the book.
만약 그가 어떻게 읽는지를 안다면, / 그는 그 책을 즐길 수 있을 텐데

혼공개념 001

실제 상황이 아닌 머릿속의 상상을 표현하는 것을 가정법이라고 해요. 특히 현재의 일에 대해 상상해 보는 것을 가정법 과거라고 하는데, **'If S + were, S + would / should / could / might +** 동사원형 ~'로 나타내고, '**S**가 ~라면, **S**가 ~ 텐데'라고 해석해요.

If I were you, I would talk to the doctor.

If you weren't a coward, you could be the greatest enemy.

What would you do if you were in my position?

He would be 88 if he were alive today.

혼공개념 002

If 문장에 **be**동사 외에 일반동사를 쓰면 가정법 과거의 다양한 표현을 할 수 있어요. '**If S** + 과거동사, **S** + **would** / **should** / **could** / **might** + 동사원형 ~'로 나타내고, '**S**가 ~한다면, **S**가 ~ 텐데'라고 해석해요.

If you went alone, you would think how nice it is.

If you didn't open this door, I would kick it open.

If you wanted it, we could stop right here.

If I took this place, you wouldn't stay here.

개념확인문제 001 다음 우리말에 맞게 영작한 것을 고르시오.

1 만약 그가 어떻게 읽는지를 안다면, 그는 그 책을 즐길 수 있을 텐데.

① If he knew how to read, he could enjoy the book.
② If he knows how to read, he could enjoy the book.

2 당신이 내 입장이라면 무엇을 할 건가요?

① What would you do if you are in my position?
② What would you do if you were in my position?

3 만약 네가 혼자 간다면, 너는 그것이 얼마나 멋진지를 생각할 텐데.

① If you went alone, you will think how nice it is.
② If you went alone, you would think how nice it is.

개념확인문제 002 다음 우리말에 맞게 순서를 바로잡아 영작하시오.

it, / we / If / wanted / stop / you / could / right here	만약 당신이 그것을 원한다면, 우리는 바로 여기서 멈출 수도 있을 텐데.

➜

혼공연습

A 다음 문장에서 밑줄 친 부분을 알맞게 해석하시오.

보기 If I were in your shoes, I'd quit the job.
만약 내가 당신의 입장이라면

1 If you wanted that knowledge, you would ask him about this.

____

2 If a miracle happened, I would be happy.

____

3 If I were you, I'd start looking for another job.

____

B 괄호 안의 단어들을 의미에 맞게 순서대로 쓰시오.

1 (you | the last person | on earth | were | If), I wouldn't marry you.

→

2 (baking | were | If | my | that bad), no one would eat my cookies.

→

3 (If | waited | you | to | apologize | a long time), it would make things worse.

→

C 다음 문장을 우리말로 해석하시오.

1 If I were you, / I'd keep away from that area at night.

→

2 If you were curious about older people, / you could broaden your horizons.

→

혼공완성

A 사진을 보고 의미에 맞게 괄호 안의 것을 순서대로 쓰시오.

1

(you | If | in the Sahara | were), you would realize the value of fresh water.

2

(you | If | business | succeeded | in), you could be rich.

B 괄호 안의 단어들을 의미에 맞게 순서대로 쓰시오.

1 If you asked politely, (refuse | he | your | couldn't | request).

➜

2 (to do | you | If | children | told | something), they wouldn't do it.

➜

3 (you | If | learn | didn't | to think), you could never learn.

➜

C ❶~❹의 괄호 안에서 어법상 알맞은 것을 골라 아래에 쓰시오.

❶ If you [try / tried] not to cry, I would tell you about it.
❷ If she only had one clue, she [can / could] solve all the problems.
❸ If I [am / were] you, I would just wait for him to come.
❹ If you didn't want to go to work, people [will / would] hire someone else.

1 ________ 2 ________ 3 ________ 4 ________

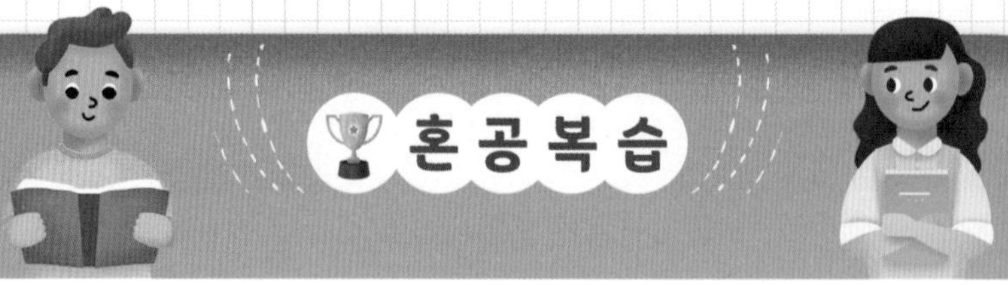

A 우리말 의미를 참고하여 빈칸을 알맞게 채우시오.

잘 모르겠다면 ···› 53페이지로

1 만약 그가 어떻게 읽는지를 안다면, 그는 그 책을 즐길 수 있을 텐데.

If he ________ how to read, he could ________ the book.

2 당신이 내 입장이라면 무엇을 할 건가요?

What ________ you do if you ________ in my position?

3 만약 네가 혼자 간다면, 너는 그것이 얼마나 멋진지를 생각할 텐데.

If you ________ alone, you would ________ how nice it is.

4 만약 당신이 그것을 원한다면, 우리는 바로 여기서 멈출 수도 있을 텐데.

If you ________ it, we ________ stop right here.

B 다음 우리말에 맞게 순서를 바로잡아 영작하시오.

잘 모르겠다면 ···› 54페이지로

1 만약 내가 당신의 입장이라면, 나는 그 직장을 그만둘 텐데.
(were | I | in | your | if | shoes), I'd quit the job.

→

2 만약 네가 지구상에 있는 마지막 사람이라면, 나는 너와 결혼하지 않을 텐데.
(you | the last person | on earth | were | if), I wouldn't marry you.

→

3 만약 네가 사과하기 위해 오래 기다린다면, 그것은 상황을 악화시킬 텐데.
(if | waited | you | to | apologize | a long time), it would make things worse.

→

4 내가 너라면, 나는 밤에 그 지역으로부터 떨어져 있을 텐데.
If I were you, (keep | that area | at night | away | I'd | from).

→

C 괄호 안의 단어들을 의미에 맞게 순서대로 쓰시오.

잘 모르겠다면 ···› 55페이지로

1 (you | if | in the Sahara | were), you would realize the value of fresh water.

➜

2 (you | if | business | succeeded | in), you could be rich.

➜

3 If you asked politely, (refuse | he | your | couldn't | request).

➜

4 (to do | you | if | children | told | something), they wouldn't do it.

➜

5 (you | if | learn | didn't | to think), you could never learn.

➜

D 다음 ❶~❹의 우리말 뜻을 적으시오.

잘 모르겠다면 ···› 55페이지로

❶ If you tried not to cry, I would tell you about it.
❷ If she only had one clue, she could solve all the problems.
❸ If I were you, I would just wait for him to come.
❹ If you didn't want to go to work, people would hire someone else.

1

2

3

4

DAY 08 가정법 과거완료

혼공기초

If I had lost the ring, / he would have really blamed me.

만약 내가 그 반지를 잃어버렸다면, / 그는 나를 정말로 비난했을 텐데

혼공개념 001

지나간 과거의 일에 대해 상상해 보는 것을 가정법 과거라고 하는데, '**If S + had been ~, S + would / should / could / might + have + p.p. ~**'로 나타내고, '**S**가 ~였다면, **S**가 ~ 했을 텐데'라고 해석해요.

If he had been angry, he certainly wouldn't have been here.

If I had been one of your family members, you would have hated me.

If you had been brave, you could have been my greatest friend.

If you had been with them, you couldn't have done anything.

혼공개념 002

If 문장에 **be**동사 외에 일반동사를 쓰면 가정법 과거완료의 다양한 표현을 할 수 있어요. **'If S + had + p.p. ~, S + would / should / could / might + have + p.p. ~**'로 나타내고, '**S**가 ~했다면, **S**가 ~ 했을 텐데'라고 해석해요.

If Len had had enough time, he could have helped me.

If I had turned the television on, it would have bothered you.

If she hadn't come to this house, it would have been worse.

If we had had the money, I would have thought about buying a new car.

개념확인문제 001 다음 우리말에 맞게 영작한 것을 고르시오.

1 만약 내가 그 반지를 잃어버렸다면, 그는 나를 정말로 비난했을 텐데.

① If I had lost the ring, he have really blamed me.
② If I had lost the ring, he would have really blamed me.

2 만약 그가 화났더라면, 그는 분명히 여기에 오지 않았을 텐데.

① If he had been angry, he certainly would have been here.
② If he had been angry, he certainly wouldn't have been here.

3 만약 Len에게 충분한 시간이 있었다면, 그는 나를 도와줄 수 있었을 텐데.

① If Len hadn't enough time, he could have helped me.
② If Len had had enough time, he could have helped me.

개념확인문제 002 다음 우리말에 맞게 순서를 바로잡아 영작하시오.

she / If / have been worse / to this house, / it / would / hadn't / come

만약 그녀가 이 집에 오지 않았다면, 상황이 더 나빠졌을 텐데.

➜

혼공연습

A 다음 문장에서 밑줄 친 부분을 알맞게 해석하시오.

> 보기
> If you had wanted to walk in the evening, I would have been with you.
> 만약 네가 저녁에 걷고 싶었더라면

1 If you had left your home, you still couldn't have done anything.

____

2 If we had found it, we would have called you.

____

3 You could have come back quickly if there had been a danger.

____

B 괄호 안의 단어들을 의미에 맞게 순서대로 쓰시오.

1 (had | any | had | If | you | questions), you would have raised your hands.

➜

2 (you | If | mentioned | her | had | name), he would have been mad at you.

➜

3 (to do | they | had | wanted | If | so), they could have changed that part.

➜

C 다음 문장을 우리말로 해석하시오.

1 Jonathan would have been disappointed / if we had left before Christmas.

➜

2 If the dough had been too sticky, / you could have added more flour.

➜

혼공완성

A 사진을 보고 의미에 맞게 괄호 안의 것을 순서대로 쓰시오.

1 

If I had had an even faster computer, (could | I | done | have | a good job).

2 

(James | If | had | down | jumped), he would have died.

B 괄호 안의 단어들을 의미에 맞게 순서대로 쓰시오.

1 (had | a person | If | those | taken | drugs), it could have been dangerous.

→

2 If you had thought it was wrong, (successful | would | nothing | have | been).

→

3 If he had trusted her, (asked | wouldn't | have | questions | he | her | so many).

→

C ❶~❹의 괄호 안에서 어법상 알맞은 것을 골라 아래에 쓰시오.

❶ If it [rained / had rained] heavily, we might not have had our picnic outside.

❷ If I had fought with my brother, you could [ask / have asked] what we were fighting about.

❸ If you [used / had used] the method, you wouldn't have wasted so much time.

❹ If you had stayed out all night in the snow, you might [froze / have frozen] to death.

1 ________ 2 ________ 3 ________ 4 ________

혼공복습

A 우리말 의미를 참고하여 빈칸을 알맞게 채우시오.

잘 모르겠다면 ···› 59페이지로

1 만약 내가 그 반지를 잃어버렸다면, 그는 나를 정말로 비난했을 텐데.

If I had ______ the ring, he would have really ______ me.

2 만약 그가 화났더라면, 그는 분명히 여기에 오지 않았을 텐데.

If he had been ______, he certainly wouldn't have ______ here.

3 만약 Len에게 충분한 시간이 있었다면, 그는 나를 도와줄 수 있었을 텐데.

If Len had had ______ time, he ______ have helped me.

4 만약 그녀가 이 집에 오지 않았다면, 상황이 더 나빠졌을 텐데.

If she ______ come to this house, it would have been ______.

B 다음 우리말에 맞게 순서를 바로잡아 영작하시오.

잘 모르겠다면 ···› 60페이지로

1 만약 네가 너의 집을 떠났더라면, 너는 여전히 어떤 것도 할 수 없었을 텐데.
(you | if | left | your | had | home), you still couldn't have done anything.

➜

2 만약 네가 질문이 있었더라면, 너는 너의 손을 들었을 텐데.
(had | any | had | if | you | questions), you would have raised your hands.

➜

3 만약 그들이 그렇게 하기를 원했더라면, 그들은 그 부분을 바꿀수 있었을 텐데.
(to do | they | had | wanted | if | so), they could have changed that part.

➜

4 만약 반죽이 너무나 달라붙었다면, 너는 밀가루를 더 넣을수도 있었을 텐데.
(the dough | had | too sticky | been | if), you could have added more flour.

➜

C 괄호 안의 단어들을 의미에 맞게 순서대로 쓰시오.

잘 모르겠다면 ···› 61페이지로

1 If I had had an even faster computer, (could | I | done | have | a good job).

➜

2 (James | if | had | down | jumped), he would have died.

➜

3 (had | a person | if | those | taken | drugs), it could have been dangerous.

➜

4 If you had thought it was wrong, (successful | would | nothing | have | been).

➜

5 If he had trusted her, (asked | wouldn't | have | questions | he | her | so many).

➜

D 다음 ❶~❹의 우리말 뜻을 적으시오.

잘 모르겠다면 ···› 61페이지로

❶ If it had rained heavily, we might not have had our picnic outside.
❷ If I had fought with my brother, you could have asked what we were fighting about.
❸ If you had used the method, you wouldn't have wasted so much time.
❹ If you had stayed out all night in the snow, you might have frozen to death.

1

2

3

4

DAY 09

if가 생략된 가정법

혼공기초

Provided I went to school, / I could study with my friends.

내가 학교에 간다면, /
나는 내 친구들과 공부할 수 있을 텐데

혼공개념 001

if가 없이도 가정법 표현을 할 수가 있어요. **if**를 생략하고 나머지 동사와 주어의 자리를 바꾸면 된답니다. **'Were it not for ~'**는 '만약 ~가 없다면', **'Had it not been for ~'**는 '만약 ~가 없었다면'으로 해석하면 된답니다.

Were it not for his help, some people would complain.

Were it not for children, this house could not be lovely.

Had it not been for his help, everyone couldn't have been safe.

**Had it not been for a cloud,
the sun would have been so bright.**

혼공개념 002

Provided로도 가정법 표현을 할 수 있어요. **'Provided** + 문장'으로 '만약 ~가 ~한다면'을 나타내고 나머지 주절 부분은 그 동안 배운 방식을 동일하게 적용하면 된답니다.

Provided you wanted to stop here, everyone wouldn't like it.

Provided you liked cooking, we could enjoy cooking class together.

Provided he went camping with his family, it would be a perfect holiday.

Provided you followed the safety rules, no one would be in danger.

개념확인문제 001 다음 우리말에 맞게 영작한 것을 고르시오.

1 내가 학교에 간다면, 나는 내 친구들과 공부할 수 있을 텐데.

① Provided I went to school, I could study with my friends.
② Provided I went to school, I couldn't study with my friends.

2 아이들이 없다면, 이 집은 사랑스러울 수 없을 텐데.

① Were it not for children, this house could not be lovely.
② Had it not been for children, this house could not be lovely.

3 그의 도움이 없었더라면, 모든 사람들이 안전할 수 없었을 텐데.

① Had it not been for his help, everyone could have been safe.
② Had it not been for his help, everyone couldn't have been safe.

개념확인문제 002 다음 우리말에 맞게 순서를 바로잡아 영작하시오.

Provided / followed / you / no one / the safety rules, / be / would / in danger

만약 네가 안전 수칙을 따른다면, 아무도 위험에 빠지지 않을 텐데.

➜

혼공연습

A 다음 문장에서 밑줄 친 부분을 알맞게 해석하시오.

보기 Were it not for the warning, everyone couldn't escape.
그 경고가 없다면

1 Were it not for hope, the heart would break.

____

2 Were it not for them, we could invite some of her friends.

____

3 Provided I ate dinner with Joe, we could be best friends.

____

B 괄호 안의 단어들을 의미에 맞게 순서대로 쓰시오.

1 (it | for | not | Were | us), their lives would be complicated.

➜

2 (Had | not | it | for | been | another responsibility), he would have played computer games all day.

➜

3 (not | it | Had | for | been | protections), the weak people wouldn't have felt comfortable.

➜

C 다음 문장을 우리말로 해석하시오.

1 Had it not been for the Spanish accent, / I would have thought he was American.

➜

2 Provided people tried to save the earth, / the environment would be better.

➜

혼공완성

A 사진을 보고 의미에 맞게 괄호 안의 것을 순서대로 쓰시오.

1 

(the snow | it | not | Were | for), the roads could be clear.

2 

(for | it | not | Had | been | the Internet), everyone couldn't have communicated with each other.

B 괄호 안의 단어들을 의미에 맞게 순서대로 쓰시오.

1 Were it not for wars, (could | peace | live | in | people).

→

2 (been | Had | fear | not | it | for), people would have fought the darkness together.

→

3 Were it not for bad people, (good | be | no | would | there | lawyers).

→

C ❶~❹의 괄호 안에서 어법상 알맞은 것을 골라 아래에 쓰시오.

❶ [Were / Had] it not been for a doubt, he would have thought of someone else as a thief.

❷ [Were / Had] it not for Jared, they might not be able to enter the building.

❸ Had it not been for the question, he wouldn't [explain / have explained] it to us.

❹ Were it not for gravity, arrows would [continue / have continued] to fly forward.

1 ______ 2 ______ 3 ______ 4 ______

혼공복습

A 우리말 의미를 참고하여 빈칸을 알맞게 채우시오.

잘 모르겠다면 ···› 65페이지로

1 내가 학교에 간다면, 나는 내 친구들과 공부할 수 있을 텐데.

Provided I ______ to school, I could ______ with my friends.

2 아이들이 없다면, 이 집은 사랑스러울 수 없을 텐데.

______ it not for children, this house could not be ______.

3 그의 도움이 없었더라면, 모든 사람들이 안전할 수 없었을 텐데.

Had it not ______ for his help, everyone ______ have been safe.

4 만약 네가 안전 수칙을 따른다면, 아무도 위험에 빠지지 않을 텐데.

Provided you ______ the safety rules, no one would be in ______.

B 다음 우리말에 맞게 순서를 바로잡아 영작하시오.

잘 모르겠다면 ···› 66페이지로

1 그 경고가 없다면, 모든 사람들이 탈출 할 수 없을 텐데.
(not | it | for | were | the warning), everyone couldn't escape.

➜

2 우리가 없다면, 그들의 삶은 복잡해질 텐데.
(it | for | not | were | us), their lives would be complicated.

➜

3 보호가 없었더라면, 약한 사람들은 편안하게 느끼지 않았을 텐데.
(not | it | had | for | been | protections), the weak people wouldn't have felt comfortable.

➜

4 사람들이 지구를 구하려 한다면, 환경은 더 나아질 텐데.
(people | provided | to save | tried | the earth), the environment would be better.

➜

C 괄호 안의 단어들을 의미에 맞게 순서대로 쓰시오.

잘 모르겠다면 ···› 67페이지로

1 (the snow | it | not | were | for), the roads could be clear.

➜

2 (for | it | not | had | been | the Internet), everyone couldn't have communicated with each other.

➜

3 Were it not for wars, (could | peace | live | in | people).

➜

4 (been | had | fear | not | it | for), people would have fought the darkness together.

➜

5 Were it not for bad people, (good | be | no | would | there | lawyers).

➜

D 다음 ❶~❹의 우리말 뜻을 적으시오.

잘 모르겠다면 ···› 67페이지로

❶ Had it not been for a doubt, he would have thought of someone else as a thief.
❷ Were it not for Jared, they might not be able to enter the building.
❸ Had it not been for the question, he wouldn't have explained it to us.
❹ Were it not for gravity, arrows would continue to fly forward.

1

2

3

4

DAY 10

혼합가정법

혼공기초

If he hadn't got tickets, / we would never be here now.

만약 그가 티켓을 사지 않았더라면, / 우리는 지금쯤 여기에 결코 없을 텐데.

혼공개념 001

현재의 일에 대해 상상해 보는 것을 가정법 과거라고 해요. 그리고 지나간 과거의 일에 대해 상상해 보는 것을 가정법 과거완료라고 배웠지요.

What would Fred do if she talked to him?

If Alex forgave his father, would he return to him?

Wouldn't it have been easier if you had told me?

She would have had a sore neck if she had stayed that way for long.

혼공개념 002

지나간 일이 사실과 달랐더라면, 지금 쯤 상황이 달라질거라고 상상해보는 경우도 있지요. 이렇게 과거와 현재가 섞인 것을 혼합가정법이라 해요.
'If S + had + p.p. ~, S + would / should / could / might + 동사원형 ~' 으로 나타내고, 주절에 **now, still**과 같은 힌트가 자주 나와요.

If he had listened to Mr. Kim's advice then, he could go to college now.

If you had been fortunate, you would not know yourself now.

If she had left then, there would never be a close relationship now.

He could be blamed now if he had made her walk home.

개념확인문제 001 다음 우리말에 맞게 영작한 것을 고르시오.

1 만약 그가 티켓을 사지 않았더라면, 우리는 지금쯤 여기에 결코 없을 텐데.

① If he didn't get tickets, we would never be here now.
② If he hadn't got tickets, we would never be here now.

2 만약 그녀가 그에게 말한다면 Fred가 무엇을 할까?

① What would Fred do if she talked to him?
② What would Fred do if she had talked to him?

3 만약 네가 운이 좋았더라면, 너는 지금쯤 너 자신을 모를 수도 있을 텐데.

① If you had been fortunate, you would know yourself now.
② If you had been fortunate, you would not know yourself now.

개념확인문제 002 다음 우리말에 맞게 순서를 바로잡아 영작하시오.

be blamed / could / if / he / now / He / her / walk / had made / home	만약 그가 그녀를 집에 걸어가게 했다면 그는 지금쯤 비난 받을 수 있을 텐데.

➜

혼공연습

A 다음 문장에서 밑줄 친 부분을 알맞게 해석하시오.

보기 If you had known the value of money, you could be rich now.
만약 네가 돈의 가치를 알았더라면,

1 If the industry hadn't developed, it would not survive now.

____

2 If you had woken me up early, I would have helped you with your homework.

____

3 If he had been in bed, he could be sicker than he expected.

____

B 괄호 안의 단어들을 의미에 맞게 순서대로 쓰시오.

1 If he had simply ignored her, (be | now | she | might | upset).

➜

2 (If | known | she | Jason | had), she would probably go earlier than him.

➜

3 (hadn't | If | born | you | been), we would be lonely.

➜

C 다음 문장을 우리말로 해석하시오.

1 If he had treated me differently, / we could get married now.

➜

2 She could drive / if someone had simply told her / where they were.

➜

혼공완성

A 사진을 보고 의미에 맞게 괄호 안의 것을 순서대로 쓰시오.

1

(had decided | to Texas | he | If | to go back), they would go together now.

2

(he | had succeeded | If | in business), he could be rich now.

B 괄호 안의 단어들을 의미에 맞게 순서대로 쓰시오.

1 If you hadn't succeeded, (have | you | given up | might | everything).

➜

2 (he | been | had | If | innocent), he would gather more information now.

➜

3 (had talked | If | she | to her family), her sister would be here to wait for her.

➜

C 다음을 혼합 가정법으로 만들려고 한다. 그때 밑줄 친 부분을 다시 쓰시오.

❶ If you <u>try</u> to cry, I would tell you about it now.
❷ If she only <u>had</u> one clue, she could solve all the problems now.
❸ If John <u>won</u> the award, I would congratulate him.
❹ If you <u>didn't want</u> to go to work, people would hire someone else now.

1 ______ 2 ______ 3 ______ 4 ______

혼공복습

A 우리말 의미를 참고하여 빈칸을 알맞게 채우시오.

잘 모르겠다면 ···› 71페이지로

1 만약 그가 티켓을 사지 않았더라면, 우리는 지금쯤 여기에 결코 없을 텐데.

If he ________ got tickets, we would never ________ here now.

2 만약 그녀가 그에게 말한다면 Fred가 무엇을 할까?

________ would Fred do if she ________ to him?

3 만약 네가 운이 좋았더라면, 너는 지금쯤 너 자신을 모를 수도 있을 텐데.

If you ________ been fortunate, you would not know yourself ________.

4 만약 그가 그녀를 집에 걸어가게 했다면 그는 지금쯤 비난 받을 수 있을 텐데.

He could be ________ now if he had made her ________ home.

B 다음 우리말에 맞게 순서를 바로잡아 영작하시오.

잘 모르겠다면 ···› 72페이지로

1 만약 네가 돈의 가치를 알았더라면, 그는 지금쯤 부자가 될 수 있을 텐데.
(you | if | the value | had known | of money), you could be rich now.

➜

2 만약 그가 단순히 그녀를 무시했다면, 그녀는 지금쯤 화낼지도 모르는데.
If he had simply ignored her, (be | now | she | might | upset).

➜

3 만약 네가 태어나지 않았더라면, 우리는 외로울 텐데.
(hadn't | If | born | you | been), we would be lonely.

➜

4 만약 그가 나를 다르게 대우했다면, 우리는 지금쯤 결혼할 수 있을 텐데.
If he had treated me differently, (get | could | married | we | now).

➜

C 괄호 안의 단어들을 의미에 맞게 순서대로 쓰시오.

잘 모르겠다면 ···› 73페이지로

1 (had decided | to Texas | he | if | to go back), they would go together now.

➜

2 (he | had succeeded | if | in business), he could be rich now.

➜

3 If you hadn't succeeded, (have | you | given up | might | everything).

➜

4 (he | been | had | if | innocent), he would gather more information now.

➜

5 (had talked | if | she | to her family), her sister would be here to wait for her.

➜

D 다음 ❶~❹의 우리말 뜻을 적으시오.

잘 모르겠다면 ···› 73페이지로

❶ If you had tried not to cry, I would tell you about it now.
❷ If she only had had one clue, she could solve all the problems now.
❸ If John had won the award, I would congratulate him.
❹ If you hadn't wanted to go to work, people would hire someone else now.

1

2

3

4

DAY 11

wish 가정법

혼공기초

I wish /
I were taller than John.

나는 소망한다 /
내가 John보다 더 키가 크기를

혼공개념 001

S + wish를 써서 현재 이룰 수 없는 소망을 표현할 수 있어요. **S + wish** 다음에 과거형 (조)동사를 쓰면 되고, '**S**는 **S**가 ~하기를 바란다' 또는 '하면 좋을 텐데'로 해석해요.

I wish you would tell me.

I wish he wouldn't lie to me.

Her husband wishes she shared her lifestyle.

My boss wishes I stood up and demanded a change.

혼공개념 002

S + wish를 써서 과거에 이룰 수 없었던 소망을 표현할 수 있어요. **S + wish** 다음에 **S + had + p.p.**를 쓰면 되고, '~했으면 좋을 텐데'로 해석해요.

I wish I had recognized my mistake.

I wish he hadn't made things worse.

I wish I had not regretted what I had done to my daughter.

The crews wish they had made things better for their work.

개념확인문제 001 다음 우리말에 맞게 영작한 것을 고르시오.

1 내가 John보다 더 키가 크면 좋을 텐데.

① I wish I were taller than John.
② I wish I will be taller than John.

2 그녀의 남편은 그녀가 그녀의 생활습관을 공유하기를 바란다.

① Her husband wishes she shared her lifestyle.
② Her husband wishes she had shared her lifestyle.

3 내가 내 실수를 알아챘으면 좋을 텐데.

① I wish I recognized my mistake.
② I wish I had recognized my mistake.

개념확인문제 002 다음 우리말에 맞게 순서를 바로잡아 영작하시오.

he / things / I / hadn't / wish / made / worse	그가 상황을 더 나쁘게 만들지 않았으면 좋을 텐데.

➜

혼공연습

A 다음 문장에서 밑줄 친 부분을 알맞게 해석하시오.

보기 He wishes <u>he asked her when he needs help</u>.
그가 도움이 필요할 때 그가 그녀에게 요청하기를

1 I wish <u>things would be different</u>.

____

2 He wishes <u>people would mention his career</u>.

____

3 She wishes <u>she focused on the past</u>.

____

B 괄호 안의 단어들을 순서에 맞게 써서 문장을 완성하시오.

1 I (had | wish | they | vacations | a lot of).

➜

2 I (she | smiled | had | at | me | wish).

➜

3 I (me | to have | wish | my parents | allowed | a cat).

➜

C 다음 문장을 우리말로 해석하시오.

1 I wished the company had done the right thing / for the environment.

➜

2 I wished I had gathered information and stories / from older people.

➜

혼공완성

A 사진을 보고 의미에 맞게 괄호 안의 것을 순서대로 쓰시오.

1 

My company (the advertisement | funny | had | wishes | looked).

2 

Mary (she | lived | near | wishes | the sea).

B 괄호 안의 단어들을 의미에 맞게 순서대로 쓰시오.

1 Joe (had | wished | time | not | waited a long | she | to apologize).

➜

2 I (sacrificed | personal lives | their | wish | had | not | my parents).

➜

3 I (broadened | my | traveling | thinking | wished | I | had | through).

➜

C 괄호 안을 참고하여 밑줄 친 부분을 다시 쓰시오.

❶ Everybody wishes they <u>are</u> perfect. (가정법 과거)
❷ My friends wished they <u>didn't</u> put their friendship in danger. (가정법 과거완료)
❸ He wishes his brother <u>had encouraged</u> people to keep going. (가정법 과거)
❹ I wish I <u>spend</u> most of my time doing things for other people. (가정법 과거완료)

1 ______ 2 ______ 3 ______ 4 ______

혼공복습

A 우리말 의미를 참고하여 빈칸을 알맞게 채우시오.

잘 모르겠다면 ···› 77페이지로

1 내가 John보다 더 키가 크면 좋을 텐데.

I ______ I ______ taller than John.

2 그녀의 남편은 그녀가 그녀의 생활습관을 공유하기를 바란다.

Her husband ______ she ______ her lifestyle.

3 내가 내 실수를 알아챘으면 좋을 텐데.

I wish I had ______ my ______.

4 그가 상황을 더 나쁘게 만들지 않았으면 좋을 텐데.

He wishes he ______ made things ______.

B 다음 우리말에 맞게 순서를 바로잡아 영작하시오.

잘 모르겠다면 ···› 78페이지로

1 그가 도움이 필요할 때 그가 그녀에게 요청하면 좋을 텐데.
her | when | he | he | he | wishes | asked | needs | help

➜

2 나는 그들이 많은 휴가를 갖기를 바란다.
had | wish | they | I | vacations | a lot of

➜

3 나는 그녀가 나에게 미소지었기를 바란다.
at | me | she | smiled | I | had | wish

➜

4 나는 내 부모님이 내가 고양이를 키우도록 허락하길 바란다.
me | to have | my parents | I | allowed | wish | a cat

➜

C 괄호 안의 단어들을 순서에 맞게 써서 문장을 완성하시오.

잘 모르겠다면 ···› 79페이지로

1 My company (the advertisement | funny | had | wishes | looked).

➔

2 Mary (she | lived | near | wishes | the sea).

➔

3 Joe (had | wished | time | not | waited a long | she | to apologize).

➔

4 I (sacrificed | personal lives | their | wish | had | not | my parents).

➔

5 I (broadened | my | traveling | thinking | wished | I | had | through).

➔

D 다음 ❶~❹의 우리말 뜻을 적으시오.

잘 모르겠다면 ···› 79페이지로

❶ Everybody wishes they were perfect.
❷ My friends wished they hadn't put their friendship in danger.
❸ He wishes his brother encouraged people to keep going.
❹ I wish I had spent most of my time doing things for other people.

1

2

3

4

DAY 12

as if 가정법

혼공기초

He acts / as if he were the owner of the house.

그는 행동한다 /
마치 그가 그 집의 주인인 것처럼

혼공개념 001

살다보면 나 또는 다른 사람이 현실이 아닌데도 자신의 이야기인듯 말하고 행동하는 경우가 있어요. 이는 '마치 ~가 ~인 것처럼 ~하다'이라는 의미의 가정법으로 표현 할 수 있는데, 이것을 **as if** 가정법 과거라고 하고 '**as if** + **S** + 과거동사 ~'로 나타낸답니다.

She cried as if she were a child.

"Thank you," Carmen said as if it were a gift.

I can remember our wedding as if it were yesterday.

His head turned slowly as if he felt the wind.

혼공개념 002

as if 가정법 역시 '마치 ~가 ~했던(였던) 것처럼 ~하다'이라는 의미로 표현할 수 있어요. 이것을 **as if** 가정법 과거완료라고 하고 '**as if** + **S** + **had** + **p.p. ~**'로 나타낸답니다.

Mom looks as if she had been sick.

He continues as if none of them had spoken.

He acts as if he had paid no attention to the news.

He was already lying down as if he had eaten.

개념확인문제 001 다음 우리말에 맞게 영작한 것을 고르시오.

1 그는 마치 그가 그 집의 주인인 것처럼 행동한다.

① He acts as if he were the owner of the house.
② He acts as if he will be the owner of the house.

2 그녀는 마치 그녀가 어린이인 것처럼 울었다.

① She cried as if she were a child.
② She cried as if she will be a child.

3 엄마는 마치 그녀가 아팠던 것처럼 보인다.

① Mom looks as if she were sick.
② Mom looks as if she had been sick.

개념확인문제 002 다음 우리말에 맞게 순서를 바로잡아 영작하시오.

none / as if / of them / He / had spoken / continues	그는 마치 그들 중 아무도 말하지 않았던 것처럼 계속한다.

➜

혼공연습

A 다음 문장에서 밑줄 친 부분을 알맞게 해석하시오.

보기 My brother is already acting as if he went to college.
마치 그가 대학을 다니는 것처럼

1 My brother is already acting as if he had gone to college.

____

2 He looks as if she had hit him in the stomach.

____

3 I worried as if I had already heard of her death.

____

B 괄호 안의 단어들을 순서에 맞게 써서 문장을 완성하시오.

1 Ashley (she | were | speaks | as if | Korean | Korean).

➜

2 Dorothy (to break | into tears | were | she | looked | as if | ready).

➜

3 It (on knives | were | so | dangerous, | as if | he | looks | walking).

➜

C 다음 문장을 우리말로 해석하시오.

1 Lena stopped for a moment / as if she had considered another plan.

➜

2 Everyone was staring at her / as if they expected her to be happy.

➜

혼공완성

A 사진을 보고 의미에 맞게 괄호 안의 것을 순서대로 쓰시오.

1

Mrs. Park (at her | shouted | were | to blame | as if | she | for the situation).

2

They (with the sticks | playing | they | as if | were | were | swords).

B 괄호 안의 단어들을 순서에 맞게 써서 문장을 완성하시오.

1 He (as if | he | spends | were | a millionaire | money).

➜

2 Her family (as if | she | were | treated | her | pregnant).

➜

3 They (each other | were | as if | they | chatting | together | had known).

➜

C 괄호 안을 참고하여 밑줄 친 부분을 다시 쓰시오.

❶ She looks pale, as if she be ill. (가정법 과거)
❷ He looked as if he saw a ghost. (가정법 과거완료)
❸ It seemed as if there is no way out. (가정법 과거)
❹ Linda speaks as if she were a boss. (가정법 과거완료)

1 ____________ 2 ____________ 3 ____________ 4 ____________

혼공복습

A 우리말 의미를 참고하여 빈칸을 알맞게 채우시오.

잘 모르겠다면 ⋯→ 83페이지로

1. 그는 마치 그가 그 집의 주인인 것처럼 행동한다.

   He ______________ as if he ______________ the owner of the house.

2. 그녀는 마치 그녀가 어린이인 것처럼 울었다.

   She ______________ as if she ______________ a child.

3. 엄마는 마치 그녀가 아팠던 것처럼 보인다.

   Mom ______________ as if she had ______________ sick.

4. 그는 마치 그들 중 아무도 말하지 않았던 것처럼 계속한다.

   He ______________ as if ______________ of them had spoken.

B 다음 우리말에 맞게 순서를 바로잡아 영작하시오.

잘 모르겠다면 ⋯→ 84페이지로

1. 그는 마치 그녀가 그의 배를 때렸던 것처럼 보인다.
   as if | she | looks | him | he | in the stomach | had hit

   →

2. Ashley는 마치 그녀가 한국인인 것처럼 한국말을 한다.
   she | were | speaks | as if | Korean | Ashley | Korean

   →

3. Dorothy는 마치 그녀가 눈물을 흘릴 준비가 된 듯 보였다.
   to break | Dorothy | into tears | were | she | looked | as if | ready

   →

4. 그것은 마치 그가 칼 위를 걷는 것처럼 너무나 위험해 보인다.
   on knives | were | so | dangerous, | as if | it | he | looks | walking

   →

C 괄호 안의 단어들을 순서에 맞게 써서 문장을 완성하시오.

잘 모르겠다면 ···› 85페이지로

1 Mrs. Park (at her | shouted | were | to blame | as if | she | for the situation).

→

2 They (with the sticks | playing | they | as if | were | were | swords).

→

3 He (as if | he | spends | were | a millionaire | money).

→

4 Her family (as if | she | were | treated | her | pregnant).

→

5 They (each other | were | as if | they | chatting | together | had known).

→

D 다음 ❶~❹의 우리말 뜻을 적으시오.

잘 모르겠다면 ···› 85페이지로

❶ She looks pale, as if she were ill.
❷ He looked as if he had seen a ghost.
❸ It seemed as if there were no way out.
❹ Linda speaks as if she had been a boss.

1

2

3

4

Part 4

기타 확장 특수구문

- Day 13 He hardly knew how it tasted.
- Day 14 Never have I seen such a strange person.
- Day 15 No one can deny the fact that fire burns.
- Day 16 I wake up in the morning and my brother in the evening.

DAY 13

부정구문

혼공기초

He hardly knew /
how it tasted.

그는 거의 몰랐다 / 그것이 어떤 맛이 나는지

혼공개념 001

no, **not**, **never** 외에도 부정을 의미하는 다양한 표현들이 있어요. **hardly**, **seldom**, **rarely**는 '거의 ~하지 않는'이라는 뜻이고, **few**, **little**는 '~가 거의 없는'는 의미로 각각 셀 수 있는 명사, 셀 수 없는 명사 앞에서 주로 쓰인답니다.

I can hardly imagine such a scene.

They rarely spoke of their future life.

In that small house, there were few secrets.

She has little water in her glass.

혼공개념 002

neither는 '둘 다 ~가 아닌', **none**은 '아무도 ~가 아닌'이라는 뜻으로 전체 부정을 의미해요. 반대로 꼭 그런 것은 아니라는 의미로 부분부정을 할 때는 **not always**(항상 ~ 인 것은 아닌), **not ~ necessarily**(반드시 ~인 것은 아닌), **not ~ all**, **not ~ every**(모두 ~인 것은 아닌)를 참고하세요.

Love can neither be bought nor sold.

Great men are not always wise.

That is not necessarily true.

Not all women like the word Ms.

개념확인문제 001 다음 우리말에 맞게 영작한 것을 고르시오.

1 그는 그것이 어떤 맛이 나는지 거의 몰랐다.

① He hardly knew how it tasted.
② He hardly didn't know how it tasted.

2 저 작은 집에, 비밀이 거의 없었다.

① In that small house, there were few secrets.
② In that small house, there were a few secrets.

3 사랑은 구매되거나 판매될 수 없다.

① Love can either be bought or sold.
② Love can neither be bought nor sold.

개념확인문제 002 다음 우리말에 맞게 순서를 바로잡아 영작하시오.

are / Great / men / not / wise / always	위대한 사람들이 항상 현명한 것은 아니다.

➜

혼공연습

A 다음 문장에서 밑줄 친 부분을 알맞게 해석하시오.

보기
I have few friends to talk with.
나는 친구들이 거의 없다

1 Her success can hardly be denied.

______

2 A little is better than none.

______

3 Childhood is not always a happy time.

______

B 괄호 안의 단어들을 순서에 맞게 써서 문장을 완성하시오.

1 He (none / knows / of / his classmates).

→ He ______.

2 I (to / go / my / seldom / hometown).

→ I ______.

3 Money (bring / not / always / does / happiness).

→ Money ______.

C 다음 문장을 우리말로 해석하시오.

1 This meat's so tough / that I can hardly chew it.

→

2 I can hardly thank you enough / for your kindness.

→

혼공완성

A 사진을 보고 주어진 단어들의 순서를 바로잡아 문장을 완성하시오.

1

hardly | There | was | a cloud | the sky | in

2

nor | were | Neither | the driver | the passengers | hurt

B 주어진 단어들의 순서를 바로잡아 문장을 완성하시오.

1 a block or two | I | than | seldom | walk | more

→

2 to run | It | on Sundays | is | economic | not | always | buses

→

3 is | Anger | not | the most | useful | reaction | necessarily

→

C ❶~❹의 괄호 안에서 어법상 알맞은 것을 골라 아래에 쓰시오.

❶ He had [little / few] experience of life.
❷ [Little / Few] places allow smoking.
❸ I have [little / few] time to talk about it.
❹ There are [little / few] reviews about the park.

1 ______ 2 ______ 3 ______ 4 ______

혼공복습

A 우리말 의미를 참고하여 빈칸을 알맞게 채우시오.

잘 모르겠다면 ⋯ 91페이지로

1 그는 그것이 어떤 맛이 나는지 거의 몰랐다.

He hardly ____________ how it ____________.

2 저 작은 집에, 비밀이 거의 없었다.

In that small house, there ____________ secrets.

3 사랑은 구매되거나 판매될 수 없다.

Love can ____________ be bought ____________ sold.

4 위대한 사람들이 항상 현명한 것은 아니다.

Great men are ____________ wise.

B 다음 우리말에 맞게 순서를 바로잡아 영작하시오.

잘 모르겠다면 ⋯ 92페이지로

1 나는 이야기를 나눌 친구들이 거의 없다.
I (friends | to talk | have | with | few).

➡

2 그는 학급 친구들을 아무도 모른다.
He (none | knows | of | the classmates).

➡

3 돈이 항상 행복을 불러오는 것은 아니다.
Money (bring | not | always | does | happiness).

➡

4 이 고기는 너무 질겨서 내가 그것을 거의 씹을 수가 없다.
This (meat | can | that | hardly | so | tough | chew | is | I | it).

➡

C 주어진 단어들의 순서를 바로잡아 문장을 완성하시오.

잘 모르겠다면 ···› 93페이지로

1 hardly | there | was | a cloud | the sky | in

➜

2 nor | were | neither | the driver | the passengers | hurt

➜

3 a block or two | I | than | seldom | walk | more

➜

4 to run | it | on Sundays | is | economic | not | always | buses

➜

5 is | anger | not | the most | useful | reaction | necessarily

➜

D 다음 ❶~❹의 우리말 뜻을 적으시오.

잘 모르겠다면 ···› 93페이지로

❶ He had little experience of life.
❷ Few places allow smoking.
❸ I have little time to talk about it.
❹ There are few reviews about the park.

1

2

3

4

DAY 14

도치구문

혼공기초

Never have I seen / such a strange person.

나는 절대 본 적이 없다 / 그렇게 이상한 사람을

혼공개념 001

부정어구를 포함한 어구를 강조하여 문장 앞에 둘 경우에 문장의 기본 어순이 **S** + **V**에서 **V** + **S**로 바뀌는 도치가 일어나요. 동사가 **be**동사인 경우는 '**be**동사 + **S**', 조동사가 있는 경우에는 '조동사 + **S** + **V**', 일반동사인 경우 '**do/does/did** + **S** + **V**'로 쓴답니다.

Never is it too late to learn.

Nothing could I think about.

Not a word did Jerry say.

Not only did he make a promise, but also he kept it.

혼공개념 002

장소나 방향을 나타내는 부사구가 문장 맨 앞에 와도 도치가 자주 일어나요. 동사가 **be**동사인 경우는 '**be**동사 + **S**', 특히 일반동사인 경우 '**V** + **S**'로 쓰이니 부정어구 도치와 차이가 좀 있다는 점을 명심해야 해요. 마지막으로 **there V** + **S**(~가 있다), **so** + **V** + **S**(**S**도 역시 그렇다), **neither**, **nor** + **V** + **S**(**S**도 역시 그렇지 않다)도 관용적으로 잘 쓰여요.

Down came the rain.

In the wallet was my card.

There lived a princess in the palace.

By the way, Alex doesn't drink and neither do I.

개념확인문제 001 다음 우리말에 맞게 영작한 것을 고르시오.

1 나는 그렇게 이상한 사람을 절대 본 적이 없다.

① Never have I seen such a strange person.
② Never I have seen such a strange person.

2 배우는 데 결코 늦은 것은 없다.

① Never it is too late to learn.
② Never is it too late to learn.

3 내 카드가 지갑 안에 있었다.

① In the wallet my card was.
② In the wallet was my card.

개념확인문제 002 다음 우리말에 맞게 순서를 바로잡아 영작하시오.

a princess / There / in / lived / the palace 궁전에 한 공주가 살았다.

➜

혼공연습

A 다음 문장에서 밑줄 친 부분을 알맞게 해석하시오.

보기 She hasn't seen him for a while, nor have I.
나도 그를 한동안 보지 못했다

1 She doesn't like to play tennis and neither do I.

____

2 Never do I wear T-shirts in summer.

____

3 Not only did I speak to her, I even got her autograph!

____

B 괄호 안의 단어들을 순서에 맞게 써서 문장을 완성하시오.

1 Hardly (my | kitchen | cook | in | do | I).

➜

2 Never (miss | practice | did | he | any reason | for).

➜

3 Here (you | some | ways | are | can improve | your English).

➜

C 다음 문장을 우리말로 해석하시오.

1 Only then did I know / riding bicycles at night was dangerous.

➜

2 Not only did we forget to turn off the lights, / but we also forgot to lock the door.

➜

혼공완성

A 사진을 보고 주어진 단어들의 순서를 바로잡아 문장을 완성하시오.

1

expect | Little | did | she | the present

2

he | his tears | Hardly | does | show

B 주어진 단어들의 순서를 바로잡아 문장을 완성하시오.

1 I | movies | Seldom | did | watch

➜

2 Never | before | have | I | about | thought | it

➜

3 spoken | they | these words | when | had | the door | Hardly | opened

➜

C ❶~❹의 밑줄 친 부분을 어법에 맞게 고쳐 쓰시오.

❶ Under the table a cat is.
❷ I enjoy Ann's company and so Martin does.
❸ Lived there an old woman called a "witch".
❹ Here the train comes!

1 ______ 2 ______ 3 ______ 4 ______

혼공복습

A 우리말 의미를 참고하여 빈칸을 알맞게 채우시오.

잘 모르겠다면 ···› 97페이지로

1 나는 그렇게 이상한 사람을 절대 본 적이 없다.

Never ________ I seen such a strange ________.

2 배우는 데 결코 늦은 것은 없다.

________ is it too late to ________.

3 내 카드가 지갑 안에 있었다.

In the ________ my card.

4 궁전에 한 공주가 살았다.

There ________ a princess in the ________.

B 다음 우리말에 맞게 순서를 바로잡아 영작하시오.

잘 모르겠다면 ···› 98페이지로

1 나는 여름에 절대 티셔츠를 입지 않는다.
(I | wear | never | do | T-shirts) in summer.

➜

2 나는 부엌에서 거의 요리를 하지 않는다.
Hardly (cook | kitchen | in | do | I | my).

➜

3 그는 어떠한 이유로도 연습을 절대 놓치지 않았다.
Never (miss | practice | did | he | any reason | for).

➜

4 여기에 당신이 당신의 영어를 향상시킬 수 있는 몇 가지 방법들이 있다.
Here (you | some | ways | are | can improve | your English).

➜

C 주어진 단어들의 순서를 바로잡아 문장을 완성하시오.

잘 모르겠다면 ···→ 99페이지로

1 expect | little | did | she | the present

→

2 he | his tears | hardly | does | show

→

3 seldom | did | I | watch | movies

→

4 never | before | have | I | about | thought | it

→

5 spoken | they | these words | when | had | the door | hardly | opened

→

D 다음 ❶~❹의 우리말 뜻을 적으시오.

잘 모르겠다면 ···→ 99페이지로

❶ Under the table is a cat.
❷ I enjoy Ann's company and so does Martin.
❸ There lived an old woman called a "witch".
❹ Here comes the train!

1

2

3

4

DAY 15

삽입/동격구문

혼공기초

No one can deny / the fact that fire burns.

아무도 부정할 수 없다 / 불이 탄다는 사실을

혼공개념 001

주로 콤마와 콤마 사이에 앞에 나온 내용에 대해 추가 설명을 해주는 것을 삽입이라고 해요. 삽입 내용을 빼고서도 나머지 부분은 하나의 완전한 문장을 이루니까, 처음에 해석이 어려울 때는 삽입 부분을 빼고 해보세요.

Mr. Park, it seems, is in his twenties.

She is, to be honest with you, not a good lawyer.

My brother, who was going to sleep, exercised until the sun came up.

He, as she told me before, missed the chance to come to his hometown.

혼공개념 002

명사나 대명사의 의미를 보충하거나 바꾸어 말하기 위해 그 뒤에 다른 명사 또는 명사어구를 두는 것을 동격이라고 해요. **fact**, **news**, **idea**, **rumor**와 같은 추상명사 뒤 **that** 다음의 내용도 앞의 명사를 자세히 풀어서 설명해주는 동격 관계랍니다.

Mr. Fox, a giant ogre, came into the room and shut the door.

He told me the fact that someone got injured.

Did you hear the news that she's going to quit her job?

He has a better idea that they can buy umbrellas at the market.

개념확인문제 001 다음 우리말에 맞게 영작한 것을 고르시오.

1 아무도 불이 탄다는 사실을 부정할 수 없다.

① No one can deny the fact that fire burns.
② No one can deny the fact which fire burns.

2 그녀는, 너에게 솔직히 말해서, 좋은 변호사가 아니다.

① She is to be honest with you not a good lawyer.
② She is, to be honest with you, not a good lawyer.

3 그는 누군가가 다쳤다는 그 사실을 나에게 말했다.

① He told me the fact that someone got injured.
② He told me the fact which someone got injured.

개념확인문제 002 다음 우리말에 맞게 순서를 바로잡아 영작하시오.

the news / Did / that / you / hear / she's / her job / going / to quit	그녀가 그녀의 직장을 그만둘 거라는 소식을 들었나요?

➜

혼공연습

A 다음 문장에서 밑줄 친 부분을 알맞게 해석하시오.

보기

Terry, a nice worker, was looking for a USB.
훌륭한 직장인인 Terry는

1 I bought a computer, which is new, for my sister.

____

2 She, a beautiful girl, laughed loudly and jumped.

____

3 Mr. Smith, my professor, makes us study English every day.

____

B 괄호 안의 단어들을 순서에 맞게 써서 문장을 완성하시오.

1 My parents, Mr. and Mrs. Kim, (want | to college | me | don't | to go).

➜

2 The idea (there | is | interesting | is | life | that | on other planets).

➜

3 I still can't believe the fact (that | died | in a helicopter crash | Kobe Bryant).

➜

C 다음 문장을 우리말로 해석하시오.

1 This shows the fact / that each organ in the body works efficiently.

➜

2 Looking at the flowers, / through the camera lens, / makes me think of nature.

➜

혼공완성

A 사진을 보고 의미에 맞게 괄호 안의 것을 순서대로 쓰시오.

1 

His pride lies in (is | that | he | a gold medal winner | the fact).

2 

This discovery disagreed with (flat | that | the world | the idea | was).

B 괄호 안의 단어들을 순서에 맞게 써서 문장을 완성하시오.

1 The idea (they | might not | that | frustrating | win | was).

→

2 Where did you get (that | the idea | doesn't | like | she | you)?

→

3 (that | heard | The fact | from | she | nothing | him) only increased her worry.

→

C ❶~❹의 괄호 안에서 어법상 알맞은 것을 골라 아래에 쓰시오.

❶ The fact [that / which] a thief broke into my house was not a good sign.
❷ Do not ride a bike [who / that] is too big for you.
❸ I heard a rumor [that / which] he cheated on the test.
❹ This is the picture [who / that] I took last year.

1 ________ 2 ________ 3 ________ 4 ________

혼공복습

A 우리말 의미를 참고하여 빈칸을 알맞게 채우시오.

잘 모르겠다면 ⋯→ 103페이지로

1 아무도 불이 탄다는 사실을 부정할 수 없다.

No one can ______ the fact that fire ______.

2 그녀는, 너에게 솔직히 말해서, 좋은 변호사가 아니다.

She is, to be ______ with you, not a good ______.

3 그는 누군가가 다쳤다는 그 사실을 나에게 말했다.

He told me the ______ that someone got ______.

4 그녀가 그녀의 직장을 그만둘 거라는 소식을 들었나요?

Did you ______ the news that she's going to ______ her job?

B 다음 우리말에 맞게 순서를 바로잡아 영작하시오.

잘 모르겠다면 ⋯→ 104페이지로

1 내 부모님이신 Mr. Kim과 Mrs. Kim은 내가 대학가는 것을 원하지 않는다.
My parents, Mr. and Mrs. Kim, (want | to college | me | don't | to go).

➜

2 다른 행성에 생명체가 있다는 생각은 흥미롭다.
The idea (there | is | is | interesting | life | that | on other planets).

➜

3 나는 여전히 Kobe Bryant가 헬리콥터 추락으로 사망했다는 사실을 믿을 수 없다.
I still can't believe the fact (that | died | in a helicopter crash | Kobe Bryant).

➜

4 이것은 몸의 각 장기가 효과적으로 일한다는 사실을 보여준다.
This shows the fact (each organ | efficiently | in | that | the body | works).

➜

C 괄호 안의 단어들을 순서에 맞게 써서 문장을 완성하시오.

잘 모르겠다면 ···› 105페이지로

1 His pride lies in (is | that | he | a gold medal winner | the fact).

➜

2 This discovery disagreed with (flat | that | the world | the idea | was).

➜

3 The idea (they | might not | that | frustrating | win | was).

➜

4 Where did you get (that | the idea | doesn't | like | she | you)?

➜

5 (that | heard | the fact | from | she | nothing | him) only increased her worry.

➜

D 다음 ❶~❹의 우리말 뜻을 적으시오.

잘 모르겠다면 ···› 105페이지로

❶ The fact that a thief broke into my house was not a good sign.
❷ Do not ride a bike that is too big for you.
❸ I heard a rumor that he cheated on the test.
❹ This is the picture that I took last year.

1

2

3

4

DAY 16

생략/공통구문

혼공기초

I wake up in the morning / and my brother in the evening.

나는 아침에 일어난다 /
그리고 내 동생은 저녁에 (일어난다)

혼공개념 001

문장의 일부를 생략하더라도 의미를 전달하는데 지장이 없을 때 생략이 일어나요. 반복되는 동사, 보어, **to** 부정사는 생략가능하고, 같은 주어가 반복될 경우 **S + be**동사도 생략한답니다.

Some went by train, some by airplane. 동사생략

She doesn't want to be late for school, but she always is. 보어생략

You may go there if you want to. to부정사 생략

Don't talk while (you are) having dinner. S + be동사 생략

혼공개념 002

문장 속에서 하나의 어구가 다른 두 개 이상의 어구에 공통의 관계를 가지는 것을 공통구문이라고 해요. 즉, 공통구문은 반복을 피하기 위해 생략을 하다보니 나오는 거랍니다. 공통어구가 앞에 있는 경우와 뒤에 있는 경우가 있어요.

She was and will be the most loved artist. **주어 (동사+동사)**

We have gathered information and stories from them. **동사 (목적어+목적어)**

He has been and will be a good student. **(동사+동사) 보어**

My mom always washes and irons our clothes. **(동사+동사) 목적어**

개념확인문제 001 다음 우리말에 맞게 영작한 것을 고르시오.

1 나는 아침에 일어나고 내 동생은 저녁에 일어난다.

① I wake up in the morning and my brother in the evening.
② I wake up in the evening and my brother in the morning.

2 저녁 식사를 하는 동안에 말을 하지 마라.

① Don't talk while having dinner.
② Don't talk while you having dinner.

3 그녀는 가장 사랑받는 아티스트였고 앞으로도 그럴 것이다.

① She was and is the most loved artist.
② She was and will be the most loved artist.

개념확인문제 002 다음 우리말에 맞게 순서를 바로잡아 영작하시오.

will / He / has / been / and / be / a good student	그는 좋은 학생이어왔고 앞으로도 그럴 것이다.

➜

혼공연습

A 다음 문장에서 밑줄 친 부분을 알맞게 해석하시오.

보기
They were tired <u>but they are not now.</u>
하지만 그들은 지금 피곤하지 않다

1. I lost <u>my wallet and my car keys</u>.

   ____

2. We <u>wish and pray for a change</u>.

   ____

3. He speaks Chinese <u>as well as or better than Zack</u>.

   ____

B 괄호 안의 단어들을 순서에 맞게 써서 문장을 완성하시오.

1. She is (the best teacher | was | to | and | me).
   → She is ______________________________ .

2. He (than | a lot | taller | a year | is | ago).
   → He ______________________________ .

3. (decisions | are | His | smart | usually | and) reasonable.
   → ______________________________ reasonable.

C 다음 문장을 우리말로 해석하시오.

1. Please pay attention to your health / as well as your career.
   →

2. Ryan used to walk 2 miles to and from school / when he was a child.
   →

혼공완성

A 사진을 보고 의미에 맞게 괄호 안의 것을 순서대로 쓰시오.

1 

Moths fly around at night, (during | but | butterflies | the day).

2 

Water is the cheapest (important | but | the most | thing).

B 괄호 안의 단어들을 의미에 맞게 순서대로 쓰시오.

1 (I | be | pretended | to | satisfied), but I wasn't.

→ , but I wasn't.

2 (didn't | marry | her | I | want | to), but I had to.

→ , but I had to.

3 (may | have | You | cookies | some) if you want to.

→ if you want to.

C ❶~❹의 문장에서 각각 생략 가능한 부분을 두 단어씩 찾아 쓰시오.

❶ You should be careful while you are driving at night.
❷ We were happy when we were at school.
❸ My grandfather is much better today than he was a week ago.
❹ He read a book while he was lying on the grass.

1 ______ 2 ______ 3 ______ 4 ______

혼공복습

A 우리말 의미를 참고하여 빈칸을 알맞게 채우시오.

잘 모르겠다면 ···› 109페이지로

1 나는 아침에 일어나고 내 동생은 저녁에 일어난다.

I wake up in the ______ and my ______ in the evening.

2 저녁 식사를 하는 동안에 말을 하지 마라.

Don't ______ while having ______.

3 그녀는 가장 사랑받는 아티스트였고 앞으로도 그럴 것이다.

She ______ and will be the most ______ artist.

4 그는 좋은 학생이어왔고 앞으로도 그럴 것이다.

He has ______ and will ______ a good student.

B 다음 우리말에 맞게 순서를 바로잡아 영작하시오.

잘 모르겠다면 ···› 110페이지로

1 나는 내 지갑과 내 자동차 열쇠를 잃어버렸다.
I lost (car | wallet | keys | and | my | my)

➜

2 그녀는 최고의 선생님이고 예전에도 나에게 그랬다.
She is (the best teacher | was | to | and | me).

➜

3 그의 결정은 보통 똑똑하고 합리적이다.
(decisions | are | his | smart | usually | and) reasonable.

➜

4 너의 직업 뿐 아니라 너의 건강에도 주의를 기울여라.
Please (to | as well as | pay | attention | your career | your health).

➜

C 괄호 안의 단어들을 의미에 맞게 순서대로 쓰시오.

잘 모르겠다면 ··· 111페이지로

1 Moths fly around at night, (during / but / butterflies / the day).

➜

2 Water is the cheapest (important / but / the most / thing).

➜

3 (I / be / pretended / to / satisfied), but I wasn't.

➜

4 (didn't / marry / her / I / want / to), but I had to.

➜

5 (may / have / you / cookies / some) if you want to.

➜

D 다음 ❶~❹의 우리말 뜻을 적으시오.

잘 모르겠다면 ··· 111페이지로

❶ You should be careful while driving at night.
❷ We were happy when at school.
❸ My grandfather is much better today than a week ago.
❹ He read a book while lying on the grass.

1

2

3

4

Part 5

실전구문독해

- **Day 17** My mom made *bibimbap* for us.
- **Day 18** Growing vegetables is good for your health.
- **Day 19** Many people like to climb to the top of the mountains.
- **Day 20** There are many good habits to make a healthy life.

DAY 17

실전구문독해 I

① 단계 독해

1 다음 글을 쓴 목적으로 가장 적절한 것은?

Are you interested in space? Then, join our club, Big Bang. We meet every Friday after school and learn about space. Come and study together.

① 전학생 소개
② 식당 사용 안내
③ 안전 수칙 제시
④ 동아리 회원 모집

2 글의 내용과 일치하지 않는 것은?

I went camping with my family. My dad set up the tent. My mom made *bibimbap* for us. After dinner, we sat around the fire, and I played the guitar. It was a special day for us.

① 나는 가족과 함께 캠핑을 갔다.
② 아버지가 텐트를 설치했다.
③ 어머니는 비빔밥을 만들었다.
④ 우리는 식사 후에 산책을 했다.

3 글의 주장으로 가장 적절한 것은?

Rivers have many benefits. We get fresh water from them. We can go to a river to go fishing, and we can even go swimming. If we want to enjoy these good things that rivers give us, we should keep them clean.

① 안전 수칙을 지키자.
② 신선한 공기를 마시자.
③ 수상 스포츠를 즐기자.
④ 강을 깨끗하게 보존하자.

4 다음 광고문에서 언급되지 않은 것은?

International Jazz Festival

Do you want to enjoy jazz from around the world?

- Date: August 13th, 2021
- Place: Seoul Grand Park
- Tickets: 8,000 won

★ Come and have fun! ☺

① 축제가 열리는 날짜
② 축제가 열리는 장소
③ 축제 입장료
④ 축제에서 제공되는 음식

② 단계 독해

1 빈칸에 들어갈 말로 가장 적절한 것은?

There are various festivals in the world. _________, there is a mud festival in Korea. At this festival, you can have fun playing in the mud. In Japan, there is a snow festival. You can take pictures of the beautiful art pieces made of snow.

① For example
② However
③ Unfortunately
④ On the other hand

2 다음에서 설명하는 'migrating birds'에 대한 내용과 일치하지 않는 것은?

Migrating birds face dangers when they migrate*. Sometimes they are hunted by other animals. The noises and lights of cities can also be dangerous to them. The worst thing is that humans destroy the places where they can live.

*migrate : 이주하다

① 이주할 때 위험에 직면한다.
② 때때로 다른 동물들에게 잡히기도 한다.
③ 도시의 소음과 불빛을 좋아한다.
④ 서식지가 인간에 의해 파괴된다.

혼공복습

A 우리말 의미를 참고하여 빈칸을 알맞게 채우시오.

잘 모르겠다면 ···› 116페이지로

1 당신은 우주에 관심이 있나요?

Are you _____ in _____?

2 우리는 매주 금요일 방과 후에 만납니다.

We _____ every Friday after _____.

3 내 아빠는 텐트를 설치했다.

My dad _____ up the _____.

4 저녁 식사 후 우리는 불 주위에 앉았다.

After _____, we _____ around the fire.

B 다음 우리말에 맞게 순서를 바로잡아 영작하시오.

잘 모르겠다면 ···› 117페이지로

1 강은 많은 이점들을 가지고 있다.
many | have | rivers | benefits

➜

2 우리는 그것들로부터 신선한 물을 얻는다.
get | them | from | we | water | fresh

➜

3 우리는 낚시하기 위해 강에 갈 수 있다.
fishing | can | to go | go | to | we | a river

➜

4 우리는 그것들을 깨끗하게 유지해야 한다.
should | we | keep | clean | them

➜

C 주어진 단어들의 순서를 바로잡아 문장을 완성하시오.

잘 모르겠다면 ···› 118페이지로

1 in | are | the world | various | there | festivals

➜

2 a mud | there | Korea | is | festival | in

➜

3 have | in | fun | can | you | playing | the mud

➜

4 is | a snow | there | festival

➜

5 take | art pieces | pictures | you | of the beautiful | can

➜

D 다음 ❶~❹의 우리말 뜻을 적으시오.

잘 모르겠다면 ···› 119페이지로

❶ Migrating birds face dangers when they migrate.
❷ Sometimes they are hunted by other animals.
❸ The noises and lights of cities can also be dangerous to them.
❹ The worst thing is that humans destroy the places where they can live.

1

2

3

4

DAY 18

실전구문독해 Ⅱ

❶단계 독해

1 다음 글을 쓴 목적으로 가장 적절한 것은?

Dear Mr. Kim,
I have something to tell you. My friends always copy my homework.
It makes me angry. What should I do?

① 수리 요청
② 고민 상담
③ 선물 구매
④ 약속 확인

2 글의 주제로 가장 적절한 것은?

Growing vegetables is good for your health. It makes your mind calm, and it gives you some exercise. You can also eat the fresh vegetables after you grow them.

① 채소를 키우는 것이 건강에 좋은 이유
② 집을 항상 청결하게 유지해야 하는 이유
③ 나무에 적절한 비료를 주어야 하는 이유
④ 건강관리를 위해 운동을 해야 하는 이유

3 글의 내용과 일치하지 <u>않는</u> 것은?

It is important to follow the safety rules when you go swimming. First, stretch before going into the water. Second, always listen to the lifeguards. Finally, only swim in permitted areas.

① 수영 안전 수칙
② 안전요원 모집
③ 수영 대회 홍보
④ 응급 구조 요령

4 환경보호를 위한 방법으로 제시되지 <u>않은</u> 것은?

SAVE THE EARTH

- We have to recycle.
- We have to save water.
- We have to reduce food waste.

① 재활용하기
② 물 절약하기
③ 대중교통 이용하기
④ 음식물 쓰레기 줄이기

❷ 단계 독해

1 글의 주제로 가장 적절한 것은?

Raising dogs is good for your health. For example, you can get some exercise when you take a walk with your dogs. When you're with your dogs, they can help you relax.

① 애완견을 키우는 것이 건강에 좋은 이유
② 집을 항상 청결하게 유지해야 하는 이유
③ 나무에 적절한 비료를 주어야 하는 이유
④ 건강관리를 위해 식단을 조절해야 하는 이유

2 밑줄 친 it이 가리키는 것으로 적절한 것은?

Salt has been in our lives for a long time. One example is that many people used salt to improve the taste of food. Gandhi also used it to lead the independence movement* in India. So, it makes our food tasty and has historical meaning.

*independence movement: 독립 운동

① 소금
② 시간
③ 예시
④ 음식 맛

혼공복습

A 우리말 의미를 참고하여 빈칸을 알맞게 채우시오.

잘 모르겠다면 ···› 122페이지로

1. 나는 당신에게 말할 어떤 것을 가지고 있다.

   I ________ something to ________ you.

2. 내 친구들이 항상 내 숙제를 베낀다.

   My ________ always ________ my homework.

3. 채소를 키우는 것은 당신의 건강에 좋다.

   Growing ________ is good for your ________.

4. 너는 그것들을 키운 다음 신선한 채소들을 또한 먹을 수 있다.

   You can also eat the ________ vegetables ________ you grow them.

B 다음 우리말에 맞게 순서를 바로잡아 영작하시오.

잘 모르겠다면 ···› 123페이지로

1. 안전수칙을 따르는 것은 중요하다.
   important | it | to follow | is | the safety rules

   ➜

2. 물에 들어가기 전에 스트레칭을 해라.
   going | before | into | stretch | the water

   ➜

3. 우리는 물을 절약해야 한다.
   save | have | to | we | water

   ➜

4. 우리는 음식물 쓰레기를 줄여야 한다.
   have | we | to | food | reduce | waste

   ➜

C 주어진 단어들의 순서를 바로잡아 문장을 완성하시오.

잘 모르겠다면 ···› 124페이지로

1 dogs | raising | is | your | good | for | health

➜

2 get | you | exercise | can | some

➜

3 take | you | with | your | a walk | dogs

➜

4 can | they | relax | help | you

➜

D 다음 ❶~❹의 우리말 뜻을 적으시오.

잘 모르겠다면 ···› 125페이지로

❶ Salt has been in our lives for a long time.
❷ One example is that many people used salt to improve the taste of food.
❸ Gandhi also used it to lead the independence movement in India.
❹ So, it makes our food tasty and has historical meaning.

1

2

3

4

DAY 19 실전구문독해 Ⅲ

❶단계 독해

1 다음 글 바로 뒤에 이어질 내용으로 가장 적절한 것은?

> I was born and grew up in Italy. I am interested in Korean music. I sometimes write about it on my blog. Here are some of my writings about Korean music.

① 한국 음악에 관한 글
② 이탈리아 여행 안내
③ Tony의 출생지 소개
④ 현명한 인터넷 사용법

2 Minsu에 관한 내용과 일치하지 <u>않는</u> 것은?

> I would like to tell you about my best friend, Minsu. He wears glasses, and he is the tallest in our class. He has one younger sister. He likes looking at the stars in the sky.

① 안경을 쓰고 있다.
② 남동생이 한 명 있다.
③ 별 보기를 좋아한다.
④ 우리 반에서 가장 키가 크다.

3 다음 글의 주제로 가장 적절한 것은?

> If you want to get good grades, it is important to set goals and study every day. It is also a good idea to study together with your friends. This will help you get good grades.

① 좋은 성적을 얻는 방법
② 건강을 잘 관리하는 방법
③ 악기를 잘 연주하는 방법
④ 친구들과 사이좋게 지내는 방법

4 전단지 내용에 언급되지 않은 것은?

> **Lost Cat**
>
> Kidi is two years old.
> She is a black cat.
> She has a white ribbon around her neck.
> Please call 546-4985 if you find her.

① 나이
② 성별
③ 성격
④ 전화번호

❷단계 독해

1 다음 글 바로 뒤에 이어질 내용으로 가장 적절한 것은?

There are a lot of mountains in the world. Many people like to climb to the top of the mountains. However, climbing mountains can be dangerous. When you climb mountains, you need to follow these safety rules.

① 세계의 높은 산
② 등산하기에 좋은 산
③ 산 정상에 오르는 이유
④ 등산할 때 지켜야 할 안전 수칙

2 글의 흐름으로 보아 빈칸에 들어갈 말로 가장 적절한 것은?

People believe that paper is not strong enough to make clothes with. ________ we can make beautiful clothes or shoes with traditional Korean paper, *hanji*. How is it possible? *Hanji* is strong because we make it from the tough bark* of the *dak* tree**.

*bark: 껍질 *dak tree: 닥나무

① So
② But
③ Then
④ Because

혼공복습

A 우리말 의미를 참고하여 빈칸을 알맞게 채우시오.

잘 모르겠다면 → 128페이지로

1. 나는 이탈리아에서 태어났고 자랐다.

   I was ______ and ______ up in Italy.

2. 나는 때때로 그것에 대해 내 블로그에 글을 쓴다.

   I sometimes ______ about it on my ______.

3. 그는 우리반에서 가장 키가 크다.

   He is the ______ in our ______.

4. 그는 하늘의 별들을 보는 것을 좋아한다.

   He ______ looking at the stars in the ______.

B 다음 우리말에 맞게 순서를 바로잡아 영작하시오.

잘 모르겠다면 → 129페이지로

1. 목표를 세우고 매일 공부하는 것이 중요하다.
   is | it | and study | important | to set goals | every day

   →

2. 너의 친구들과 함께 공부하는 것은 또한 좋은 생각이다.
   is | also | with your friends | a good idea | it | together | to study

   →

3. 이것은 네가 좋은 성적을 받도록 도와줄 것이다.
   help | will | you | get | good | this | grades

   →

4. 그녀는 그녀의 목 주위에 하얀색 리본을 착용하고 있다.
   neck | has | her | around | a white | she | ribbon

   →

C 주어진 단어들의 순서를 바로잡아 문장을 완성하시오.

잘 모르겠다면 …→ 130페이지로

1 are | the world | there | mountains | a lot of | in

→

2 people | many | to climb | like | of the mountains | to the top

→

3 mountains | climbing | be | can | dangerous

→

4 climb | mountains | you

→

5 safety | need to | follow | these | you | rules

→

D 다음 ❶~❹의 우리말 뜻을 적으시오.

잘 모르겠다면 …→ 131페이지로

❶ People believe that paper is not strong enough to make clothes with.
❷ But we can make beautiful clothes or shoes with traditional Korean paper, *hanji*.
❸ How is it possible?
❹ *Hanji* is strong because we make it from the tough bark of the *dak* tree.

1

2

3

4

DAY 20

실전구문독해 Ⅳ

① 단계 독해

1 다음 중 밑줄 친 them이 가리키는 것으로 적절한 것은?

> Jisu makes delicious cookies. She sometimes brings her cookies to class and gives <u>them</u> to us. I ate her cookies yesterday. They were so good!

① books
② cookies
③ classes
④ friends

2 다음 글을 쓴 목적으로 가장 적절한 것은?

> I bought a shirt for my dad at your shop yesterday, but he doesn't like the color. Can I exchange it for a black one? Please let me know if it is possible. Thanks.

① 친구를 추천하기 위해
② 숙소를 예약하기 위해
③ 셔츠를 교환하기 위해
④ 파티에 초대하기 위해

3 Jim Abbott에 관한 다음 글의 내용에서 알 수 없는 것은?

> Jim Abbott was born on September 19, 1967, in America without a right hand, but he really liked baseball. He practiced every day to be a good baseball player. Later, Jim Abbott became a famous baseball player.

① 태어난 해
② 태어난 나라
③ 졸업한 학교
④ 좋아한 운동

4 생일 초대장을 보고 알 수 없는 것은?

> **Birthday Party**
>
> You're invited to Mary's birthday party!
>
> • Date: March 20
> • Time: 5 p.m.
> • Place: Happy Restaurant
>
> ★ Call me at 008-123-5467 if you can come.

① 시간
② 장소
③ 연락처
④ 참석 인원

② 단계 독해

1 다음 글의 주제로 가장 알맞은 것은?

There are various types of table manners around the world. Here are two examples. One is that, in China, some people leave some food on their plates to be polite. The other is that, in India, most people eat food using their right hand.

① 인도 영화 산업의 발전
② 한국 음식의 조리 방법
③ 교통 법규 지키기의 중요성
④ 세계 여러 나라의 다양한 식사예절

2 글의 제목으로 가장 적절한 것은?

There are many good habits to make a healthy life. Getting up early, having breakfast every morning, and going jogging are good examples. If you keep habits like these, you can be healthy and happy.

① 신속한 요리 방법
② 간편한 조깅 복장
③ 적당한 아침 기상 시간
④ 건강을 위한 좋은 습관

혼공복습

A 우리말 의미를 참고하여 빈칸을 알맞게 채우시오.

잘 모르겠다면 … 134페이지로

1 그녀는 때때로 그녀의 쿠키를 반에 가져와서 그것들을 우리들에게 준다.

She sometimes ________ her cookies to class and ________ them to us.

2 나는 그녀의 쿠키들을 어제 먹었다.

I ________ her cookies ________.

3 나는 어제 당신의 가게에서 내 아빠를 위한 셔츠를 샀다.

I ________ a shirt for my ________ at your shop yesterday.

4 제가 그것을 검정색으로 교환할 수 있을까요?

Can I ________ it for a ________ one?

B 다음 우리말에 맞게 순서를 바로잡아 영작하시오.

잘 모르겠다면 … 135페이지로

1 Jim Abbott은 9월 19일에 태어났다.
born | was | Jim Abbott | September 19 | on

→

2 그는 훌륭한 야구 선수가 되기 위해 매일 연습했다.
every day | practiced | a good | to be | he | baseball player

→

3 Jim Abbott은 유명한 야구 선수가 되었다.
became | baseball player | a famous | Jim Abbott

→

4 너는 Mary의 생일 파티에 초대되었다.
Mary's | you're | invited | to | birthday party

→

C 주어진 단어들의 순서를 바로잡아 문장을 완성하시오.

잘 모르겠다면 ···› 136페이지로

1 are | there | types of | table manners | various | around the world

➜

2 two | here | are | examples

➜

3 people | some food | some | leave | to be polite | on their plates

➜

4 eat | people | using | food | their | right hand | most

➜

D 다음 ❶~❸의 우리말 뜻을 적으시오.

잘 모르겠다면 ···› 137페이지로

❶ There are many good habits to make a healthy life.
❷ Getting up early, having breakfast every morning, and going jogging are good examples.
❸ If you keep habits like these, you can be healthy and happy.

1

2

3

Part 6

Special
56문장

★ [1 ~ 56] 다음 사진과 우리말을 보고 영작하시오.

1

Carmen은 토마토 하나를 집어들었고 그것의 껍질을 까기 시작했다.

12쪽

2

그것은 아주 똑똑한 포유류이다.

15쪽

3

그들은 그것을 사용하는 것을 중단하기로 결정했다.

15쪽

4

사람들이 더 잘 일하도록 돕는 바로 그것은 그 기술이다.

18쪽

5

Tom이 매일 읽는 것은 바로 그 신문이다.

21쪽

6

내가 캠핑을 같이 갔던 것은 바로 내 가족이었다.

21쪽

7 

여기서 가게까지는 4 마일이다.

24쪽

8 

그녀의 방 안은 어둡다.

27쪽

9 

어제는 꽁꽁 얼게 추웠다.

27쪽

10 

그는 그가 고등학교에 있는 동안 화산에 관심이 생겼다.

32쪽

11 

그는 아침에 모두가 잠에서 깰 때까지 잤다.

35쪽

12 

그 문을 열자마자, 나는 신선한 커피 향기를 맡았다.

35쪽

13 

그들은 그들의 계획이 발견되었기 때문에 화가 났다.

38쪽

14 

그 케익은 너무나 맛있어서 모두가 그것을 좋아했다.

41쪽

15 

그것은 너무 많아서 사람들이 저녁으로 먹을 수 있었다.

41쪽

16 

비록 그가 새 신발을 신고 있었음에도 불구하고, 그는 빨리 달릴 수 없었다.

44쪽

17 

비록 그것이 아름다움에도 불구하고 그녀는 이 집을 싫어했다.

47쪽

18 

비록 그가 화나는 중이었음에도 불구하고, 그의 목소리는 계속 차분했다.

47쪽

19

만약 그가 어떻게 읽는지를 안다면, 그는 그 책을 즐길 수 있을 텐데.

52쪽

20

만약 당신이 사하라 사막에 있다면, 당신은 신선한 물의 가치를 깨달을 텐데.

55쪽

21

만약 당신이 사업에서 성공하면, 당신은 부유해질 수 있을 텐데.

55쪽

22

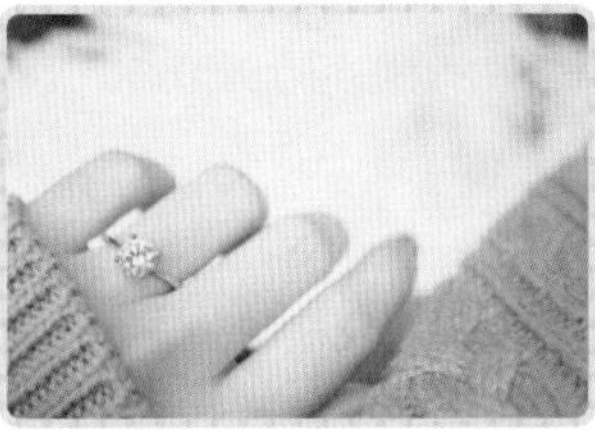

만약 내가 그 반지를 잃어버렸다면, 그는 나를 정말로 비난했을 텐데.

58쪽

23

만약 내가 훨씬 더 빠른 컴퓨터를 가졌더라면, 나는 잘 할 수 있었을 텐데.

61쪽

24

만약 James가 뛰어내렸다면, 그는 죽었을 텐데.

61쪽

25

내가 학교에 간다면, 나는 내 친구들과 공부할 수 있을 텐데. (Provided)

64쪽

26

눈이 없다면, 그 길들은 깨끗해질 수 있을 텐데. (Were it)

67쪽

27

인터넷이 없었더라면, 모든 사람들은 서로 소통할 수 없었을 텐데.

67쪽

28

만약 그가 티켓을 사지 않았더라면, 우리는 지금쯤 여기에 결코 없을 텐데.

70쪽

29

만약 그가 텍사스로 다시 돌아가기를 결심했다면, 그들은 지금쯤 함께 갈 텐데.

73쪽

30

만약 그가 사업에서 성공했더라면, 그는 지금쯤 부유할 수 있을 텐데.

73쪽

31

나는 내가 John보다 더 키가 크기를 바란다.

76쪽

32

내 회사는 그 광고가 웃기게 보였기를 바란다.

79쪽

33

Mary는 그녀가 바다 근처에 살기를 바란다.

79쪽

34

그는 마치 그가 그 집의 주인인 것처럼 행동한다.

82쪽

35

Mrs. Park은 마치 그녀가 그 상황에 대해 비난받아야 할 것처럼 그녀에게 소리쳤다.

85쪽

36

그들은 마치 그것들이 칼인 것처럼 막대기로 놀고 있는 중이었다.

85쪽

37 

그는 그것이 어떤 맛이 나는지 거의 몰랐다.

90쪽

38 

하늘에는 거의 구름 한 점 없었다.

93쪽

39 

운전자와 승객들 누구도 다치지 않았다.

93쪽

40 

나는 그렇게 이상한 사람을 절대 본 적이 없다.

96쪽

41 

그녀는 그 선물을 거의 예상하지 못했다.

99쪽

42 

그는 그의 눈물을 거의 보이지 않는다.

99쪽

43

아무도 불이 탄다는 사실을 부정할 수 없다.

102쪽

44

그의 자부심은 그가 금메달 수상자라는 사실에 있다.

105쪽

45

그 발견은 세상이 평평하다는 생각과는 일치하지 않았다.

105쪽

46

나는 아침에 일어나고 내 동생은 저녁에 일어난다.

108쪽

47

나방들은 밤에 날아다니지만, 나비들은 낮 동안 날아다닌다.

111쪽

48

물은 가장 싸지만, 가장 중요한 것이다.

111쪽

49 

한국에는 머드 축제가 있다.

118쪽

50 

이주하는 새들은 그들이 이주할 때 위험에 직면한다.

119쪽

51 

개들을 키우는 것은 당신의 건강에 좋다.

124쪽

52 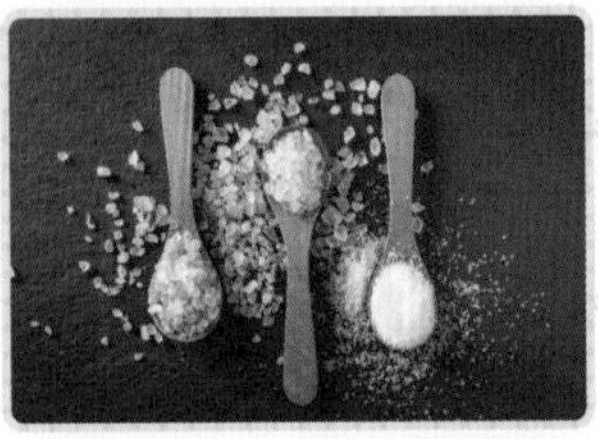

소금은 오랫동안 우리 삶에 있어왔다.

125쪽

53 

많은 사람들은 산들의 꼭대기에 오르는 것을 좋아한다.

130쪽

54 

우리들은 전통 한국 종이인 한지로 아름다운 옷이나 신발을 만들 수 있다.

131쪽

55

전 세계에는 다양한 유형의 식사 매너가 있다.

136쪽

56

건강한 삶을 만들기 위한 많은 좋은 습관들이 있다.

137쪽

Answers
정답

DAY 01 대명사 it

개념확인문제 001 본문 13쪽

1 ① 2 ① 3 ①

개념확인문제 002 본문 13쪽

I don't know why it matters.

혼공연습 본문 14쪽

A ① 모자
② 고양이
③ 공

B ① won't spend it
② was not a good question
③ is a beautiful place

C ① 그녀가 그것을 말하고 난 후에 / 그녀는 그것을 후회했다
② 나는 그것을 공부하려고 애썼다 / 하지만 할 수 없었다

혼공완성 본문 15쪽

A ① It is a very smart mammal.
② They decided to stop using it.

B ① What a pretty sound it made!
② The big question was how to end it.
③ It was the first money that he had ever had.

C ① Of course V was the same.
② Why don't you share V?
③ You just have to act like you already know V.
④ I only hope V wasn't poisonous.

혼공복습 본문 16쪽

A ① tomato, it
② hat, looked
③ cooked, fun
④ why, matters

B ① She picked up the ball and threw it to me.
② James won't spend it.
③ It is a beautiful place.
④ I tried to study it, but I couldn't.

C ① It is a very smart mammal.
② They decided to stop using it.
③ What a pretty sound it made!
④ The big question was how to end it.
⑤ It was the first money that he had ever had.

D ① 물론 그것은 똑같은 것이었다.
② 그것을 공유하는게 어때?
③ 당신은 그저 당신이 이미 그것을 알고있는 것처럼 행동해야 한다.
④ 나는 그것이 독이 없었기를 바랄 뿐이다.

DAY 02 강조구문의 it

개념확인문제 001 본문 19쪽

1 ② 2 ① 3 ①

개념확인문제 002 본문 19쪽

It is at the stadium where the concert will take place.

혼공연습 본문 20쪽

A ① 명동이 한국에서 유명했던 때는
② 그녀가 문 앞에서 보았던 사람은
③ 그가 자랑스러워 했던 것은

B ① that helped him win a competition
② who tried to climb these huge mountains
③ who went to Africa to take care of many people

C ① 바로 그이다/ 내가 너에게 말하고 싶은 사람은
② 바로 그 요리 수업이다/ Tommy가 참가하고 싶은 것은

혼공완성 본문 21쪽

A ① that Tom reads every day
② who I went camping with

B ① rules that you have to follow
② song that I'm interested in
③ classroom that we have to clean up

C ① It is before laundry V people should check the amount of clothes.
② It was Lena V liked looking at the stars in the sky.
③ It is snow V these beautiful art pieces are made of.
④ It is Koreans V make food and share it with other people.

혼공복습 (본문 22쪽)

A ① game, buy
② years, participated
③ stopped, said
④ stadium, take

B ① where the police officer found a dog
② that helped him win a competition
③ who went to Africa to take care of many people
④ that Tommy wants to join

C ① that Tom reads every day
② who I went camping with
③ rules that you have to follow
④ song that I'm interested in
⑤ classroom that we have to clean up

D ① 사람들이 옷의 양을 확인해야 할 때는 바로 세탁 전이다.
② 하늘에 있는 별들을 보는 것을 좋아하는 사람은 바로 Lena였다.
③ 이 아름다운 예술 작품들은 바로 눈으로 만들어졌다.
④ 음식을 만들고 그것을 다른 사람들과 나누는 사람들은 바로 한국인들이다.

DAY 03 비인칭 주어 it

개념확인문제 001 (본문 25쪽)

1 ① 2 ② 3 ②

개념확인문제 002 (본문 25쪽)

It's too bright, so I can't see anything.

혼공연습 (본문 26쪽)

A ① 날씨
② 요일
③ 거리

B ① snows till February
② rains a lot in Vancouver / rains in Vancouver a lot
③ it far from here

C ① 비가 올 수도 있다 / 그러나 하여간 나는 밖으로 나갈 것이다
② 날씨가 흐릴지도 모른다 / 그렇지만 괜찮다

혼공완성 (본문 27쪽)

A ① It is dark in her room.
② It was freezing yesterday.

B ① It takes an hour to get there on foot.
② It usually takes three hours from Busan to Seoul.
③ It takes about five hours by train.

C ① What day is it today? V
② It was so hot in Atlanta.
③ It's going to rain.
④ It's sunny today.

혼공복습 (본문 28쪽)

A ① four, here
② almost, afternoon
③ far, it
④ bright, see

B ① It was Monday yesterday.
② It rains a lot in Vancouver.
It rains in Vancouver a lot.
③ Is it far from here?
④ It might be cloudy, but that's okay.

C ① It is dark in her room.
② It was freezing yesterday.
③ It takes an hour to get there on foot.
④ It usually takes three hours from Busan to Seoul.
⑤ It takes about five hours by train.

D ① 오늘은 무슨 요일이니?
② Atlanta는 매우 더웠다.
③ 비가 올 것이다.
④ 오늘은 화창하다.

DAY 04 시간/조건의 접속사

개념확인문제 001 (본문 33쪽)

1 ② 2 ① 3 ②

개념확인문제 002 (본문 33쪽)

I don't care as long as you love me.

혼공연습 본문 34쪽

A ① 그가 소년이었을 때
② 내가 저녁식사를 마친 후
③ 내가 살아있는 한

B ① If you cannot bite
② When he answered
③ since we met

C ① 그가 떠난 후에/ 그녀는 여행가방 중 하나를 들었고/ 그것을 침대 위에 두었다
② 사람들은 밤에 거리를 쓸었다/ 기계가 그들을 대체할 때까지

혼공완성 본문 35쪽

A ① until everybody woke up in the morning / in the morning until everybody woke up
② As soon as I opened the door

B ① when they are going out
② until the school bell rings
③ until it was closed by the Romans

C ① + ② Call me if it's a real emergency.
③ + ④ My baby sister never cries unless she is hungry.

혼공복습 본문 36쪽

A ① volcanoes, while
② must, while
③ unless, terrible
④ care, long

B ① as long as I live
② If you cannot bite
③ since we met
④ until a machine replaced them

C ① until everybody woke up in the morning / in the morning until everybody woke up
② As soon as I opened the door
③ when they are going out
④ until the school bell rings
⑤ until it was closed by the Romans

D ① 나에게 전화해 줘.
② 그것은 진짜 위급상황이다.
③ 나의 어린 여동생은 결코 울지 않는다.
④ 그녀는 배가 고프다.

DAY 05 원인/결과/목적의 접속사

개념확인문제 001 본문 39쪽

1 ② 2 ① 3 ①

개념확인문제 002 본문 39쪽

It was so dark that I couldn't see his expression.

혼공연습 본문 40쪽

A ① 우리가 많은 제품들을 사기 때문에
② 너무 빨라서 그녀는 생각할 시간이 없었다
③ 우리가 원하는 것을 할 수 있기 위해서

B ① that I couldn't wait until midnight
② that we couldn't go out
③ so that everyone can eat

C ① 이것이 그들이 아는 유일한 힘이기 때문에 / 그것은 그들이 존중하는 유일한 힘이다
② 수천 명의 사람들이 질병을 연구한다 / 왜냐하면 그들은 그것들을 치료하고 싶기 때문이다

혼공완성 본문 41쪽

A ① so delicious that everyone liked it
② so much that people could eat for dinner

B ① because I like to see my friends
② so long that it was difficult to catch her
③ since the palace was accessible without booking

C ① so ② such ③ so ④ such

혼공복습 본문 42쪽

A ① angry, discovered
② sorry, cried
③ organized, find
④ dark, expression

B ① that she didn't have time to think
② that I couldn't wait until midnight
③ that we couldn't go out
④ so that everyone can eat

C ① so delicious that everyone liked it
② so much that people could eat for dinner
③ because I like to see my friends
④ so long that it was difficult to catch her

⑤ since the palace was accessible without booking

D ① 나는 너무 걱정이 되어서 어떤 것도 생각할 수 없었다.
② 우리는 너무나 좋은 시간을 보내는 중이었기 때문에 더 오래 머물기로 결심했다.
③ 너무 늦어서 사람들이 포기하기 시작하는 중이다.
④ 그의 계획은 너무나 성공적이었기 때문에 심지어 그의 경쟁자들도 그를 칭찬했다.

DAY 06 대조의 접속사

개념확인문제 001 본문 45쪽

1 ② 2 ① 3 ②

개념확인문제 002 본문 45쪽

Even if they are rich, they will live simply.

혼공연습 본문 46쪽

A ① 심지어 그것이 매우 소리가 크지 않았음에도 불구하고
② 다른 사람들이 정장을 입었던 반면에
③ 내가 가버렸음에도 불구하고

B ① Although I could not raise my arms
② though he was talking to his grandparents
③ even if your voice shakes

C ① 우리는 예전의 우리보다 낫다 / 비록 아무것도 만들어지지 않았음에도 불구하고

② 그들은 단지 스페인어만 한다 / 반면에 우리는 여러 개의 언어를 할 수 있다

혼공완성 본문 47쪽

A ① though it was beautiful
② Even though he was getting angry

B ① Though her favorite color was red
② while researchers work in the daytime
③ Even though the issue was not discussed

C ① if
② though
③ if
④ though

혼공복습 본문 48쪽

A ① Though(Although), wearing
② studies, languages
③ took, afford
④ if, live

B ① while others wore formal clothes
② Although I could not raise my arms
③ though he was talking to his grandparents
④ while we can speak several languages

C ① though it was beautiful
② Even though he was getting angry
③ Though her favorite color was red
④ while researchers work in the daytime
⑤ Even though the issue was not discussed

D ① 심지어 내가 한 시간이 있더라도 나는 쇼핑하러 나가지 않을 것이다.
② 심지어 그들이 그녀를 배신했음에도 불구하고 그녀는 그들에게 미소지었다.
③ 심지어 그가 그의 직업을 잃더라도 그는 그의 경력을 계속 이어나갈 것이다.
④ 심지어 나는 여러 겹의 옷을 입었음에도 불구하고 감기에 걸렸다.

DAY 07 가정법 과거

개념확인문제 001 본문 53쪽

1 ① 2 ② 3 ②

개념확인문제 002 본문 53쪽

If you wanted it, we could stop right here.

혼공연습 본문 54쪽

A ① 만약 당신이 그 지식을 원한다면
② 만약 기적이 일어난다면
③ 나는 다른 직업을 알아보기 시작할 텐데

B ① If you were the last person on earth
② If my baking were that bad
③ If you waited a long time to apologize

C ① 내가 너라면, / 나는 밤에 그 지역으로부터 떨어져 있을 텐데
② 네가 노인들에 대해 궁금해한다면, / 너는 너의 시야를 넓힐 수 있을 텐데

혼공완성 본문 55쪽

A ① If you were in the Sahara
② If you succeeded in business

B ① he couldn't refuse your request
② If you told children to do something /
If you told children something to do
③ If you didn't learn to think

C ① tried ② could ③ were ④ would

혼공복습 본문 56쪽

A ① knew, enjoy
② would, were
③ went, think
④ wanted, could

B ① If I were in your shoes
② If you were the last person on earth
③ If you waited a long time to apologize
④ I'd keep away from that area at night

C ① If you were in the Sahara
② If you succeeded in business
③ he couldn't refuse your request
④ If you told children to do something /
If you told children something to do
⑤ If you didn't learn to think

D ① 만약 네가 울지 않으려고 노력한다면, 나는 너에게 그것에 대해 말해줄 텐데
② 만약 그녀가 단서를 하나라도 가지고 있다면, 그녀는 모든 문제를 풀 수 있을 텐데
③ 내가 너라면, 나는 그냥 그가 오기를 기다릴 텐데
④ 네가 출근하는 것을 원하지 않으면, 사람들이 다른 누군가를 고용할 텐데

DAY 08 가정법 과거완료

개념확인문제 001 본문 59쪽

1 ② 2 ② 3 ②

개념확인문제 002 본문 59쪽

If she hadn't come to this house, it would have been worse.

혼공연습 본문 60쪽

A ① 만약 네가 너의 집을 떠났더라면
② 만약 우리가 그것을 발견했다면
③ 네가 빨리 돌아올 수 있었을 텐데

B ① If you had had any questions
② If you had mentioned her name
③ If they had wanted to do so

C ① Jonathan은 실망했었을 텐데, / 만약 우리가 크리스마스 전에 떠났다면
② 만약 반죽이 너무 달라붙었다면, / 너는 밀가루를 더 넣을 수도 있었을 텐데

혼공완성 본문 61쪽

A ① I could have done a good job
② If James had jumped down

B ① If a person had taken those drugs
② nothing would have been successful
③ he wouldn't have asked her so many questions

C ① had rained ② have asked ③ had used
④ have frozen

혼공복습 본문 62쪽

A ① lost, blamed
② angry, come
③ enough, could
④ hadn't, worse

B ① If you had left your home
② If you had had any questions
③ If they had wanted to do so
④ If the dough had been too sticky

C ① I could have done a good job
② If James had jumped down
③ If a person had taken those drugs
④ nothing would have been successful
⑤ he wouldn't have asked her so many questions

D ① 만약 비가 심하게 왔다면, 우리는 밖으로 소풍을 가지 못했을 텐데.
② 만약 내가 나의 남동생과 싸웠더라면, 너는 무엇때문에 우리가 싸웠는지 물어볼 수 있었을 텐데.
③ 만약 네가 그 방법을 사용했었다면, 너는 그렇게 많은 시간을 낭비하지 않았을 텐데.

④ 만약 눈 속에서 네가 밤을 새웠다면, 너는 얼어 죽었을지도 모를 텐데.

DAY 09 if가 생략된 가정법

개념확인문제 001 본문 65쪽

1 ① 2 ① 3 ②

개념확인문제 002 본문 65쪽

Provided you followed the safety rules, no one would be in danger.

혼공연습 본문 66쪽

A ① 희망이 없다면
② 그들이 없다면
③ 만약 내가 Joe와 저녁식사를 한다면

B ① Were it not for us
② Had it not been for another responsibility
③ Had it not been for protections

C ① 스페인 억양이 없었다면, / 나는 그를 미국인으로 생각했을 텐데
② 사람들이 지구를 구하려 한다면, / 환경은 더 나아질 텐데

혼공완성 본문 67쪽

A ① Were it not for the snow
② Had it not been for the Internet

B ① people could live in peace
② Had it not been for fear
③ there would be no good lawyers

C ① Had ② Were ③ have explained
④ continue

혼공복습 본문 68쪽

A ① went, study
② Were, lovely
③ been, couldn't
④ followed, danger

B ① Were it not for the warning
② Were it not for us
③ Had it not been for protections
④ Provided people tried to save the earth

C ① Were it not for the snow
② Had it not been for the Internet
③ people could live in peace
④ Had it not been for fear
⑤ there would be no good lawyers

D ① 하나도 의심이 없었다면, 그는 다른 누군가를 도둑으로 생각했을 텐데
② Jared가 없다면, 그들은 문을 통과하지 못 할 텐데.
③ 질문이 없었다면, 그는 그것을 우리에게 설명하지 않았을 텐데.
④ 중력이 없다면, 화살은 계속해서 앞을 향해 날아갈 텐데.

DAY 10 혼합가정법

개념확인문제 001 본문 71쪽

1 ② 2 ① 3 ②

개념확인문제 002 본문 71쪽

He could be blamed now if he had made her walk home.

혼공연습 본문 72쪽

A ① 그것은 지금 살아남지 않을 텐데
② 만약 네가 나를 일찍 깨웠다면
③ 그는 그가 예상했던 것 보다 더 아플 수 있을 텐데

B ① she might be upset now
② If she had known Jason
③ If you hadn't been born

C ① 그가 나를 다르게 대우했다면, / 우리는 지금쯤 결혼할 수 있을 텐데
② 그녀가 운전해서 갈 수 있을 텐데 / 만약 누군가가 단지 그녀에게 말해줬다면 / 그들이 어디 있는지를

혼공완성 본문 73쪽

A ① If he had decided to go back to Texas
② If he had succeeded in business

B ① you might have given up everything
② If he had been innocent
③ If she had talked to her family

C ① had tried ② had had ③ had won
④ hadn't wanted

혼공복습 본문 74쪽

A ① hadn't, be
② What, talked
③ had, now
④ blamed, walk

B ① If you had known the value of money
② she might be upset now
③ If you hadn't been born
④ we could get married now

C ① If he had decided to go back to Texas
② If he had succeeded in business
③ you might have given up everything
④ If he had been innocent
⑤ If she had talked to her family

D ① 네가 울지 않으려고 노력했다면, 나는 지금쯤 너에게 그것에 대해 말해줄 텐데.
② 그녀가 단지 단서 하나를 가지고 있었다면, 그녀는 지금쯤 모든 문제를 다 풀 수 있을 텐데.
③ John이 그 상을 탔더라면, 나는 그에게 축하를 해줄 텐데.
④ 네가 출근하는 것을 원하지 않았다면, 사람들이 지금쯤 다른 누군가를 고용할 텐데.

DAY 11 wish 가정법

개념확인문제 001 본문 77쪽

1 ① 2 ① 3 ②

개념확인문제 002 본문 77쪽

I wish he hadn't made things worse.

혼공연습 본문 78쪽

A ① 상황이 달라지기를
② 사람들이 그의 경력을 언급하기를
③ 그녀가 과거에 집중하기를

B ① wish they had a lot of vacations
② wish she had smiled at me
③ wish my parents allowed me to have a cat

C ① 회사가 옳은 일을 했다면 좋았을 텐데 / 환경을 위해서
② 내가 정보와 이야기들을 모았다면 좋았을 텐데 / 나이드신 분들로부터

혼공완성 본문 79쪽

A ① wishes the advertisement had looked funny
② wishes she lived near the sea

B ① wished she had not waited a long time to apologize
② wish my parents had not sacrificed their personal lives
③ wished I had broadened my thinking through traveling

C ① were ② hadn't ③ encouraged
④ had spent

혼공복습 본문 80쪽

A ① wish, were
② wishes, shared
③ recognized, mistake
④ hadn't, worse

B ① He wishes he asked her when he needs help.
② I wish they had a lot of vacations.
③ I wish she had smiled at me.
④ I wish my parents allowed me to have a cat.

C ① wishes the advertisement had looked funny
② wishes she lived near the sea
③ wished she had not waited a long time to apologize
④ wish my parents had not sacrificed their personal lives
⑤ wished I had broadened my thinking through traveling

D ① 모든 사람은 그들이 완벽하기를 바란다.
② 나의 친구들은 그들이 우정을 위험에 빠뜨리지 않았기를 바랐다.
③ 그는 사람들이 계속 하도록 그의 형이 격려하기를 바란다.
④ 나의 대부분의 시간을 다른 사람을 위해서 무엇인가를 하는데 보냈다면 좋을 텐데.

DAY 12 as if 가정법

개념확인문제 001 본문 83쪽

1 ① 2 ① 3 ②

개념확인문제 002 본문 83쪽

He continues as if none of them had spoken.

혼공연습 본문 84쪽

A ① 마치 그가 대학을 다녔던 것처럼
② 마치 그녀가 그의 배를 때렸던 것처럼
③ 마치 내가 그녀의 죽음을 이미 들었던 것처럼

B ① speaks Korean as if she were Korean
② looked as if she were ready to break into tears
③ looks so dangerous, as if he were walking on knives

C ① Lena는 잠시 멈췄다 / 마치 그녀가 다른 계획을 고려했던 것처럼
② 모두 그녀를 보는 중이었다 / 마치 그들이 그녀가 행복하기를 기대하는 것처럼

혼공완성 본문 85쪽

A ① shouted at her as if she were to blame for the situation
② were playing with the sticks as if they were swords

B ① spends money as if he were a millionaire
② treated her as if she were pregnant
③ were chatting together as if they had known each other

C ① were ② had seen ③ were ④ had been

혼공복습 본문 86쪽

A ① acts, were
② cried, were
③ looks, been
④ continues, none

B ① He looks as if she had hit him in the stomach.
② Ashley speaks Korean as if she were Korean.
③ Dorothy looked as if she were ready to break into tears.
④ It looks so dangerous, as if he were walking on knives.

C ① shouted at her as if she were to blame for the situation
② were playing with the sticks as if they were swords
③ spends money as if he were a millionaire
④ treated her as if she were pregnant
⑤ were chatting together as if they had known each other

D ① 그녀는 마치 그녀가 아픈 것처럼 창백해 보인다.
② 그는 마치 귀신을 봤던 것처럼 보였다.
③ 마치 나가는 길이 없는 것처럼 보였다.
④ Linda는 마치 그녀가 대장이었던 것처럼 말한다.

DAY 13 부정구문

개념확인문제 001 본문 91쪽

1 ① 2 ① 3 ②

개념확인문제 002 본문 91쪽

Great men are not always wise.

혼공연습 본문 92쪽

A ① 거의 부인될 수 없다
② 없는 것 보다 낫다
③ 항상 행복한 시간은 아니다

B ① knows none of his classmates
② seldom go to my hometown
③ does not always bring happiness

C ① 이 고기는 너무 질기다 / 나는 거의 그것을 씹을 수가 없다
② 나는 거의 너에게 충분히 감사할 수 없다 / 너의 친절에 대해

혼공완성 본문 93쪽

A ① There was hardly a cloud in the sky.
② Neither the driver nor the passengers were hurt.

B ① I seldom walk more than a block or two.
② It is not always economic to run buses on Sundays.

③ Anger is not necessarily the most useful reaction.

C ① little ② few ③ little ④ few

혼공복습 본문 94쪽

A ① knew, tasted
② were, few
③ neither, nor
④ not, always

B ① have few friends to talk with
② knows none of the classmates
③ does not always bring happiness
④ meat is so tough that I can hardly chew it

C ① There was hardly a cloud in the sky.
② Neither the driver nor the passengers were hurt.
③ I seldom walk more than a block or two.
④ It is not always economic to run buses on Sundays.
⑤ Anger is not necessarily the most useful reaction.

D ① 그는 인생의 경험이 거의 없었다.
② 흡연을 허용하는 장소는 거의 없다.
③ 나는 그것에 대해 말할 시간이 거의 없다.
④ 그 공원에 대한 후기는 거의 없다.

DAY 14 도치구문

개념확인문제 001 본문 97쪽

1 ① 2 ② 3 ②

개념확인문제 002 본문 97쪽

There lived a princess in the palace.

혼공연습 본문 98쪽

A ① 나도 테니스하는 것을 좋아하지 않는다
② 나는 절대 티셔츠를 입지 않는다
③ 나는 그녀에게 말을 걸었을 뿐만 아니라

B ① do I cook in my kitchen
② did he miss practice for any reason
③ are some ways you can improve your English

C ① 그때서야 나는 알았다/ 밤에 자전거를 타는 것이 위험하다는 것을
② 우리는 불을 끄는 것을 잊었을 뿐만 아니라/ 우리는 문을 잠그는 것도 잊었다

혼공완성 본문 99쪽

A ① Little did she expect the present.
② Hardly does he show his tears.

B ① Seldom did I watch movies.
② Never have I thought about it before.
③ Hardly had they spoken these words when the door opened.

C ① is a cat ② does Martin ③ There lived
④ comes the train

혼공복습 본문 100쪽

A ① have, person
② Never, learn
③ wallet, was
④ lived, palace

B ① Never do I wear T-shirts
② do I cook in my kitchen
③ did he miss practice for any reason
④ are some ways you can improve your English

C ① Little did she expect the present.
② Hardly does he show his tears.
③ Seldom did I watch movies.
④ Never have I thought about it before.
⑤ Hardly had they spoken these words when the door opened.

D ① 탁자 아래에 고양이가 있다.
② 나는 Ann과 동행하는 것이 즐겁고 Martin도 즐거워한다.
③ "마녀"라고 불리는 노파가 살았습니다.
④ 기차가 온다!

DAY 15 삽입/동격구문

개념확인문제 001 본문 103쪽

1 ① 2 ② 3 ①

개념확인문제 002 본문 103쪽

Did you hear the news that she's going to quit her job?

혼공연습 본문 104쪽

A ① 나는 새로운 컴퓨터를 샀다
② 아름다운 소녀인 그녀는
③ 나의 교수님인 Mr. Smith는

B ① don't want me to go to college
② that there is life on other planets is interesting
③ that Kobe Bryant died in a helicopter crash

C ① 이것은 사실을 보여준다/ 몸의 각 장기가 효과적으로 일한다는
② 꽃을 보는 것은/ 카메라 렌즈를 통해서/ 내가 자연을 생각하게 만든다

혼공완성 본문 105쪽

A ① the fact that he is a gold medal winner
② the idea that the world was flat

B ① that they might not win was frustrating
② the idea that she doesn't like you
③ The fact that she heard nothing from him

C ① that ② that ③ that ④ that

혼공복습 본문 106쪽

A ① deny, burns
② honest, lawyer
③ fact, injured
④ hear, quit

B ① don't want me to go to college
② that there is life on other planets is interesting
③ that Kobe Bryant died in a helicopter crash
④ that each organ in the body works efficiently

C ① the fact that he is a gold medal winner
② the idea that the world was flat
③ that they might not win was frustrating
④ the idea that she doesn't like you
⑤ The fact that she heard nothing from him

D ① 도둑이 나의 집에 침입했다는 사실은 좋은 신호가 아니었다.
② 너한테 너무 큰 자전거를 타지 말아라.
③ 나는 그가 시험에서 부정행위를 했다는 소문을 들었다.
④ 이것은 내가 작년에 찍은 사진이다.

DAY 16 생략/공통구문

개념확인문제 001 본문 109쪽

1 ① 2 ① 3 ②

개념확인문제 002 본문 109쪽

He has been and will be a good student.

혼공연습 본문 110쪽

A ① 내 지갑과 내 자동차 열쇠를
② 변화를 소망하고 기도한다
③ Zack만큼 잘하거나 혹은 더 잘

B ① and was the best teacher to me
② is a lot taller than a year ago
③ His decisions are usually smart and

C ① 부디 너의 건강에 주의를 기울여라/ 너의 직업 뿐 아니라
② Ryan은 2마일을 걸어서 등하교를 하곤했다/ 그가 어렸을 때

혼공완성 본문 111쪽

A ① but butterflies during the day
② but the most important thing

B ① I pretended to be satisfied
② I didn't want to marry her
③ You may have some cookies

C ① you are ② we were ③ he was
④ he was

혼공복습 본문 112쪽

A ① morning, brother
② talk, dinner
③ was, loved
④ been, be

B ① my wallet and my car keys
② and was the best teacher to me
③ His decisions are usually smart and
④ pay attention to your health as well as your career

C ① but butterflies during the day
② but the most important thing
③ I pretended to be satisfied
④ I didn't want to marry her

⑤ You may have some cookies

D ① 너는 밤에 운전하는 동안에는 조심해야 한다.
② 우리는 학교에 있을 때 행복했다.
③ 나의 할아버지는 일주일 전보다 오늘 훨씬 더 좋으시다.
④ 그는 풀 위에 누워서 책을 읽었다.

DAY 17 실전구문독해 Ⅰ

1단계 독해 (본문 116쪽)

1 ④ 2 ④ 3 ④ 4 ④

2단계 독해 (본문 118쪽)

1 ① 2 ③

혼공복습 (본문 120쪽)

A ① interested, space
② meet, school
③ set, tent
④ dinner, sat

B ① Rivers have many benefits.
② We get fresh water from them.
③ We can go to a river to go fishing.
④ We should keep them clean.

C ① There are various festivals in the world.
② There is a mud festival in Korea.
③ You can have fun playing in the mud.
④ There is a snow festival.
⑤ You can take pictures of the beautiful art pieces.

D ① 이주하는 새들은 이주할 때 위험에 직면한다.
② 때때로 그들은 다른 동물들에게 잡히기도 한다.
③ 도시의 소음과 불빛은 그들에게 위험할 수도 있다.
④ 가장 나쁜 것은 인간이 그들이 살 수 있는 곳을 파괴하는 것이다.

DAY 18 실전구문독해 Ⅱ

1단계 독해 (본문 122쪽)

1 ② 2 ① 3 ① 4 ③

2단계 독해 (본문 124쪽)

1 ① 2 ①

혼공복습 (본문 126쪽)

A ① have, tell
② friends, copy
③ vegetables, health
④ fresh, after

B ① It is important to follow the safety rules.
② Stretch before going into the water.
③ We have to save water.
④ We have to reduce food waste.

C ① Raising dogs is good for your health.
② You can get some exercise.
③ You take a walk with your dogs.
④ They can help you relax.

D ① 소금은 우리의 삶에 오랫동안 있어왔다.
② 하나의 예는 많은 사람들이 음식의 맛을 향상시키기 위해 소금을 사용했다는 것이다.
③ Gandhi 또한 인도에서 독립 운동을 이끌기 위해 그것을 사용했다.
④ 그래서 그것은 우리의 음식을 맛있게 만들고 역사적인 의미를 가지고 있다.

DAY 19 실전구문독해 Ⅲ

1단계 독해 (본문 128쪽)

1 ① 2 ② 3 ① 4 ③

2단계 독해 (본문 130쪽)

1 ④ 2 ②

혼공복습 (본문 132쪽)

A ① born, grew
② write, blog
③ tallest, class
④ likes, sky

B ① It is important to set goals and study every day.
② It is also a good idea to study together with your friends.
③ This will help you get good grades.

④ She has a white ribbon around her neck.

C ① There are a lot of mountains in the world.
② Many people like to climb to the top of the mountains.
③ Climbing mountains can be dangerous.
④ You climb mountains.
⑤ You need to follow these safety rules.

D ① 사람들은 종이가 옷을 만들 만큼 충분히 강하지 않다고 믿는다.
② 하지만 우리는 한국 전통 종이인 한지로 아름다운 옷이나 신발을 만들 수 있다.
③ 어떻게 그것이 가능할까?
④ 우리가 닥나무의 질긴 껍질로 한지를 만들기 때문에 한지는 튼튼하다.

DAY 20 실전구문독해 Ⅳ

1단계 독해 (본문 134쪽)

1 ② 2 ③ 3 ③ 4 ④

2단계 독해 (본문 136쪽)

1 ④ 2 ④

혼공복습 (본문 138쪽)

A ① brings, gives
② ate, yesterday
③ bought, dad
④ exchange, black

B ① Jim Abbott was born on September 19.
② He practiced every day to be a good baseball player.
③ Jim Abbott became a famous baseball player.
④ You're invited to Mary's birthday party.

C ① There are various types of table manners around the world.
② Here are two examples.
③ Some people leave some food on their plates to be polite.
④ Most people eat food using their right hand.

D ① 건강한 삶을 만드는 많은 좋은 습관들이 있다.
② 일찍 일어나는 것, 매일 아침 식사를 하는 것, 조깅을 하러가는 것은 좋은 예들이다.
③ 만약에 네가 이러한 습관들을 잘 지키면, 너는 건강하고 행복해 질 수 있을 것이다.

★ Special 56 문장 ★ (본문 142쪽)

1 Carmen picked up a tomato and started peeling it.
2 It is a very smart mammal.
3 They decided to stop using it.
4 It is the technology that helps people to work better.
5 It is the newspaper that Tom reads every day.
6 It was my family who I went camping with.
7 It's four miles from here to the store.
8 It is dark in her room.
9 It was freezing yesterday.
10 He became interested in volcanoes while he was in high school.
11 He slept until everybody woke up in the morning.
12 As soon as I opened the door, I smelled the aroma of fresh coffee.
13 They were angry because their plans had been discovered.
14 The cake was so delicious that everyone liked it.
15 It was so much that people could eat for dinner.
16 Though he was wearing new shoes, he couldn't run fast.
17 She hated this house though it was beautiful.
18 Even though he was getting angry, his voice remained calm.
19 If he knew how to read, he could enjoy the book.
20 If you were in the Sahara, you would realize the value of fresh water.
21 If you succeeded in business, you could be rich.
22 If I had lost the ring, he would have really blamed me.
23 If I had had an even faster computer, I could have done a good job.
24 If James had jumped down, he would have died.
25 Provided I went to school, I could study with my friends.

26 Were it not for the snow, the roads could be clear.
27 Had it not been for the Internet, everyone couldn't have communicated with each other.
28 If he hadn't got tickets, we would never be here now.
29 If he had decided to go back to Texas, they would go together now.
30 If he had succeeded in business, he could be rich now.
31 I wish I were taller than John.
32 My company wishes the advertisement had looked funny.
33 Mary wishes she lived near the sea.
34 He acts as if he were the owner of the house.
35 Mrs. Park shouted at her as if she were to blame for the situation.
36 They were playing with the sticks as if they were swords.
37 He hardly knew how it tasted.
38 There was hardly a cloud in the sky.
39 Neither the driver nor the passengers were hurt.
40 Never have I seen such a strange person.
41 Little did she expect the present.
42 Hardly does he show his tears.
43 No one can deny the fact that fire burns.
44 His pride lies in the fact that he is the gold medal winner.
45 The discovery disagreed with the idea that the world was flat.
46 I wake up in the morning and my brother in the evening.
47 Moths fly around at night, but butterflies during the day.
48 Water is the cheapest but the most important thing.
49 There is a mud festival in Korea.
50 Migrating birds face dangers when they migrate.
51 Raising dogs is good for your health.
52 Salt has been in our lives for a long time.
53 Many people like to climb to the top of the mountains.
54 We can make beautiful clothes or shoes with traditional Korean paper, *hanji*.
55 There are various types of table manners around the world.
56 There are many good habits to make a healthy life.

★ Memo ★

★ Memo ★